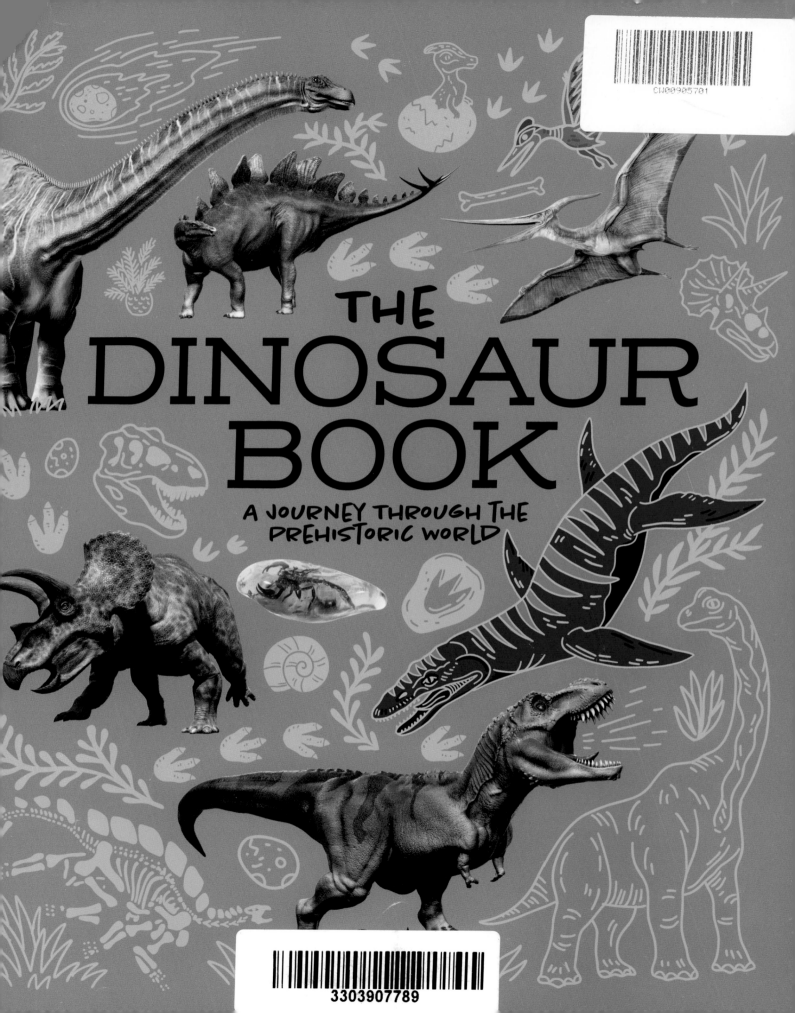

THE DINOSAUR BOOK

A JOURNEY THROUGH THE PREHISTORIC WORLD

Picture Credits:
Key: b–bottom, t–top, c–centre, l–left, r–right
Stefano Azzalin: 11r, 13t, 18–19, 24cr, 33tl, 40cr, 42–43, 46–47, 51t, 67bl, 68c, 75tl, 83t, 86b, 92–93, 96–97, 114cr, 114–115, 116bl, 118c, 120cl, 120–121, 122l, 124br, 124–125;
Martin Bustamante: 6br, 14c, 16l, 21tr, 22–23, 28br, 30–31, 40–41, 42c, 78l, 82–83, 90–91, 94bl, 106c, 110l, 110–111, 112c, 112–113; **Juan Calle:** 19br, 24–25, 57cr, 70–71, 78–79; **Mat Edwards:** profile box icons, 1, 4–5, 6–7, 8–9, 10–11, 12–13, 14–15, 16–17, 20–21, 26–27, 28–29, 36–37, 38–39, 44–45, 48–49, 50–51, 52–53, 54–55, 58–59, 60–61, 62–63, 64–65, 66–67, 72–73, 74c, 74–75, 76–77, 80–81, 84–85, 86–87, 94–95, 98–99, 102–103, 104–105, 106–107, 108–109, 118–119; **Rudolf Farkas:** 56–57; **Colin Howard:** 25cl;
Kunal Kundu: 34–35, 57tl, 68–69, 88–89, 116–117; **Jerry Pyke:** 8cr, 23bl, 34tr, 88b; **Shutterstock:** 11b MikhailSh, 12cr Didier Descouens, 18cr Catmando, 31t Michael Rosskothen, 31bl Catmando, 32cr Ozja, 37t Linda Bucklin, 38b Catmando, 41t watthanachai, 43r Herschel Hoffmeyer, 44cr cjchiker, 49t Linda Bucklin, 53r CTR Photos, 58tr Adwo, 60bl Elenarts, 63br Warpaint, 70cr Valentyna Chukhlyebova, 73br Michael Rosskothen, 76l Warpaint, 84l Ozja, 92b, 98b Linda Bucklin, 102c Valentyna Chukhlyebova, 121t Catmando, 125cr Warpaint; **Parwinder Singh:** 66b, 104b; **Val Walerczuk:** 32–33, 81bl, 108l, 122–123; **Wikimedia Commons:** 7bl Ghedoghedo, 9t mrwynd/ Denver Museum of Science and Nature, 15tr Didier Descouens/Peabody Museum of Natural History, 17t Didier Descouens, 20b Kevmin/Burke Museum/Museum of the Rockies, 22l Funk Monk/Lindsay E Zanno, 29cr Funk Monk/philosophygeek, 34c Gastón Cuello/Museo Paleontológico Egidio Feruglio, 36c CaptMondo/Royal Ontario Museum, 45cr D Gordon and E Robertson/Royal Ontario Museum, 46c Carol Abraczinskas, Paul C Sereno/ZooKeys, 46br Daderot/University of California Museum of Paleontology, 49bl Joseph Smit/biodiversitylibrary.org, 51cr Aimé Rutot, 54cr FunkMonk, 58bl William Diller Matthew, 62c Conty and Ballista/Oxford University Museum, 64l UNC Sea Grant College Program, 65t Tim Evanson/Museum of the Rockies, 68bl Daderot/Naturmuseum Senckenberg, 71br Kumiko, 72bl Christophe Hendrickx/American Museum of Natural History, 77 Tim Evanson/Museum of the Rockies, 79t American Museum of Natural History, 80l Eduard Solà/Royal Belgian Institute of Natural Sciences, 82l Allie Caulfield/Los Angeles Museum of Natural History, 84br John R Horner and Mark B Goodwin, 86tr Dmitry Bogdanov/FunkMonk, 89tr Joseph Dinkel, 91t Drow Male/Natural History Museum, London, 92tr Daderot/Natural History Museum of Utah, 95br H Zell/Natural History Museum, Berlin, 96cr Mariana Ruiz Lady of Hats, 98cr Ryan Somma, 100c JT Csotonyi, 101tr Eden, Janine, and Jim, NYC, 103t Victoria M Arbour and Philip J Currie/American Museum of Natural History, 106br Ra'ike/Museum am Löwentor, Stuttgart, 109br Daderot/Royal Ontario Museum, 111r Smart Destinations/Harvard Museum of Natural History, 113c Tai Kubo, Mark T Mitchell, and Donald M Henderson/Smokeybjb, 115br Ghedoghedo/Royal Belgian Institute of Natural Sciences, 116tr James Erxleben/ British Museum, 119cl Ghedoghedo/Museo di Storia Naturale di Verona, 123r Régine Debatty.

ARCTURUS

This edition published in 2024 by Arcturus Publishing Limited
26/27 Bickels Yard, 151–153 Bermondsey Street,
London SE1 3HA

ISBN: 978-1-3988-3573-3
CH005152NT
Supplier 29, Date 0824, PI 00005984

Author: Clare Hibbert
Cover artist: Lizzy Doyle
Editors: Joe Harris and Clare Hibbert @ Hollow Pond
Designer: Amy McSimpson @ Hollow Pond

Printed in China

CONTENTS

The Dinosaur Age

Dinosaurs appeared around 225 million years ago (mya) and ruled the land for over 160 million years. At the same time (the Mesozoic Era), marine reptiles and pterosaurs ruled the oceans and skies.

This family tree shows when the dinosaurs in this book (chapters 1–5) appeared and how they were related. As new fossils are found, paleontologists often change their minds about the groupings.

Dinosaurs suddenly died out 65 mya, along with marine reptiles, pterosaurs and many other animals. A huge meteorite probably hit Earth, throwing up dust that blocked out the Sun for months.

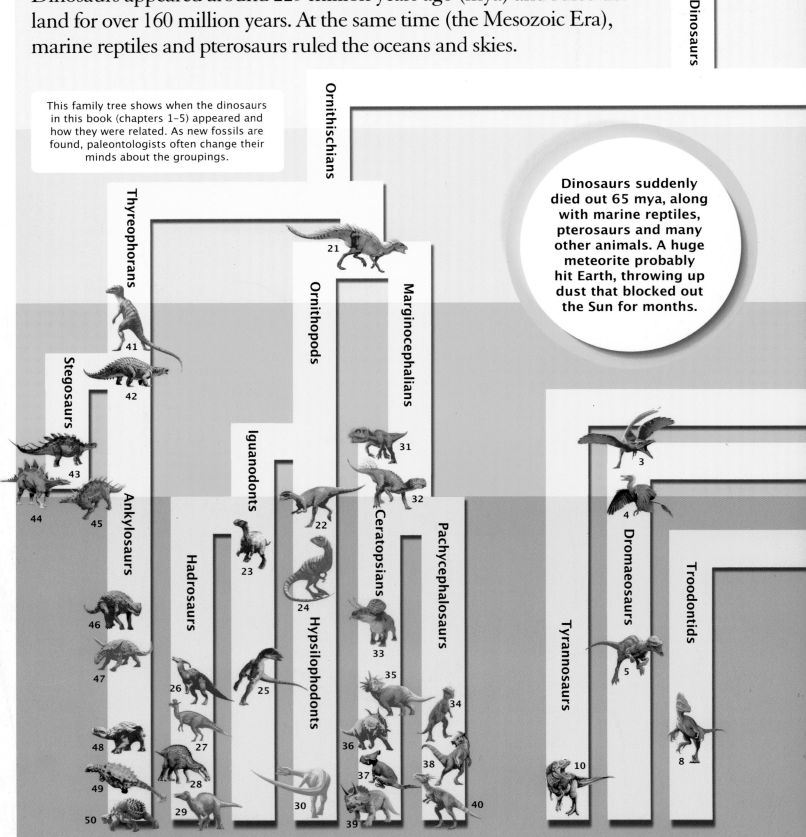

PERIOD	TRIASSIC	JURASSIC	CRETACEOUS	AGE OF MAMMALS

MILLIONS OF YEARS AGO

251   231   206   145   65   present

Name: *Herrerasaurus*
(Her–RARE–uh–SAWR–us)
Family: Herrerasauridae
Height: 1.5 m (5 ft)
Length: 3 m (10 ft)
Weight: 210 kg (460 lb)

DINOSAUR PROFILE

Herrerasaurus used sight and sound to find prey.

This small, stocky reptile is a rhynchosaur. Its beaky mouth clips off plant stems to eat.

Front legs had grasping, curved claws.

The first complete *Herrerasaurus* skull was discovered in 1988. Before then, paleontologists had to work from fragments.

Allosaurus

Late Jurassic North America was home to *Allosaurus*, one of the best-known carnivorous dinosaurs. Paleontologists have more fossils of *Allosaurus* to study than of any other dinosaur. The first were found in the late 19th century. The bones had honeycombed holes to make them lighter, just like birds' bones today. *Allosaurus* was given its name, which means "different lizard," because no other dinosaur fossils at that time had those holes.

Famous Fossils

Swiss fossil hunter Kirby Siber and his team of dinosaur experts were responsible for finding two of the most complete *Allosaurus* specimens. Discovered in Wyoming in 1991, the skeleton of "Big Al" is 95 percent complete. The specimen was not fully grown and probably died of a bone infection. Five years later the team found an even more complete *Allosaurus*, which they named "Big Al Two." Its skull showed signs of injuries that had healed.

On Location

There are five known species of *Allosaurus*. Four were discovered in the Morrison Formation, a band of Late Jurassic rock in the western United States. The other comes from western Portugal's Lourinhã Formation.

The long tail stuck out behind for balance.

PERIOD	TRIASSIC	JURASSIC	CRETACEOUS	AGE OF MAMMALS
		152		

MILLIONS OF YEARS AGO: 251 · 206 · 145 · 65 · present

Name: *Allosaurus*
(AL–uh–SAWR–us)
Family: Allosauridae
Height: 5 m (16.5 ft)
Length: 12 m (40 ft)
Weight: 2.7 tonnes (3 tons)

DINOSAUR PROFILE

DID YOU KNOW? *Allosaurus* was very common. Up to **three-quarters** of the theropod fossils from the U.S.A.'s Morrison Formation belong to *Allosaurus*.

This *Allosaurus* skeleton is posed to take on *Stegosaurus* (pages 92–93).

Thick, sturdy legs supported its heavy bulk.

Allosaurus had long claws for gripping flesh.

Allosaurus fed on carrion or its own kills.

Archaeopteryx

Birdlike *Archaeopteryx* lived in what is now southern Germany around 150 million years ago. For many years it was the oldest-known bird, but in recent decades earlier feathered dinosaurs have been discovered. *Archaeopteryx* had flight feathers for gliding.

Germany in the Late Jurassic

The landscape where *Archaeopteryx* lived was made up of low-lying islands among bodies of water, called lagoons. These lagoons had become separated from the nearby Tethys Ocean. When they dried up, the mud turned into limestone. Creatures that had sunk to the bottom were preserved as fossils.

Some experts think *Archaeopteryx*'s wrists were not flexible enough for powered flight.

Archaeopteryx was about the same size as a raven. It hunted frogs, lizards, dragonflies, and beetles.

Archaeopteryx's teeth were sharp and cone-shaped.

Flapping its wings while it was running helped *Archaeopteryx* to move faster.

150

MILLIONS OF YEARS AGO

251 206 145 65 present

Name: *Archaeopteryx*
(Ar–kee–OP–ter–ix)
Family: Archaeopterygidae
Length: 30 cm (12 in)
Wingspan: 50 cm (20 in)
Weight: 1 kg (2.2 lb)

DINOSAUR PROFILE

Mesozoic dragonflies were huge, with wingspans up to 75 cm (30 in).

Archaeopteryx means "ancient wing."

Early Bird

The first feathered dinosaur ever discovered, *Archaeopteryx* was nicknamed the "first bird." It was clearly an early ancestor of birds because of its wing and tail feathers. However, it also had reptilian features—a long, bony tail, large hand claws, and jaws lined with sharp teeth.

An *Archaeopteryx* skeleton preserved in limestone

DID YOU KNOW? The first *Archaeopteryx* fossil was found in 1859—the same year that Charles Darwin published his theory of **evolution** by natural selection.

11

Microraptor

The trees of Early Cretaceous China were home to *Microraptor*, a small, four-winged dromaeosaur. Like *Archaeopteryx*, it is one of the missing links between dinosaurs and birds. It probably used its wings to glide and parachute, rather than truly fly.

Microraptor stretched out its limbs and tail to be as aerodynamic as possible.

Speedy Killer

Microraptor was an opportunist—in other words, it ate whatever prey came its way. It must have been an agile, speedy hunter. *Microraptor* fossils show the remains of small mammals, birds, and even fish inside its gut. One bird meal had been swallowed whole.

Skeleton Specimens

Microraptor was discovered in 2000 in the Jiufotang Formation, a layer of rock in Liaoning, northeastern China. During the Early Cretaceous, Liaoning was warm and swampy. Rocks from that time contain the fossilized remains of many creatures, including other feathered dinosaurs. So far, hundreds of *Microraptor* specimens have been found.

Microraptor had fine, delicate bones.

PERIOD	TRIASSIC	JURASSIC	CRETACEOUS	AGE OF MAMMALS
MILLIONS OF YEARS AGO	251	206	145 ● 120	65 present

Name: *Microraptor* (MY-kro-rap-tor)
Family: Dromaeosauridae
Length: 65 cm (2.1 ft)
Wingspan: 92 cm (36 in)
Weight: 650 g (1.4 lb)

DINOSAUR PROFILE

DID YOU KNOW? *Microraptor* was not the only **four-winged** dinosaur. *Changyuraptor*, also from Cretaceous China, was the largest, measuring 1.3 m (4.3 ft) from nose to tail.

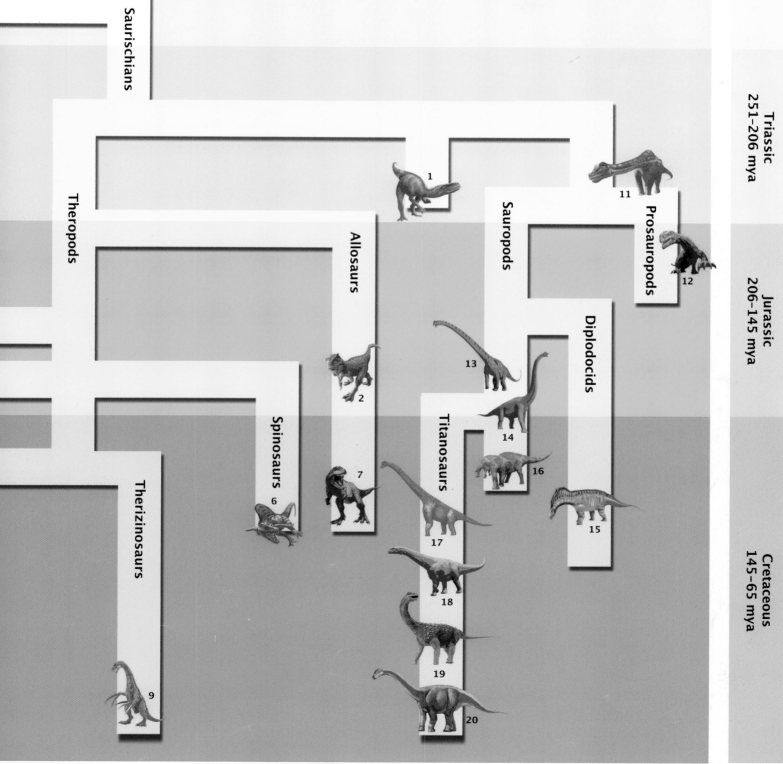

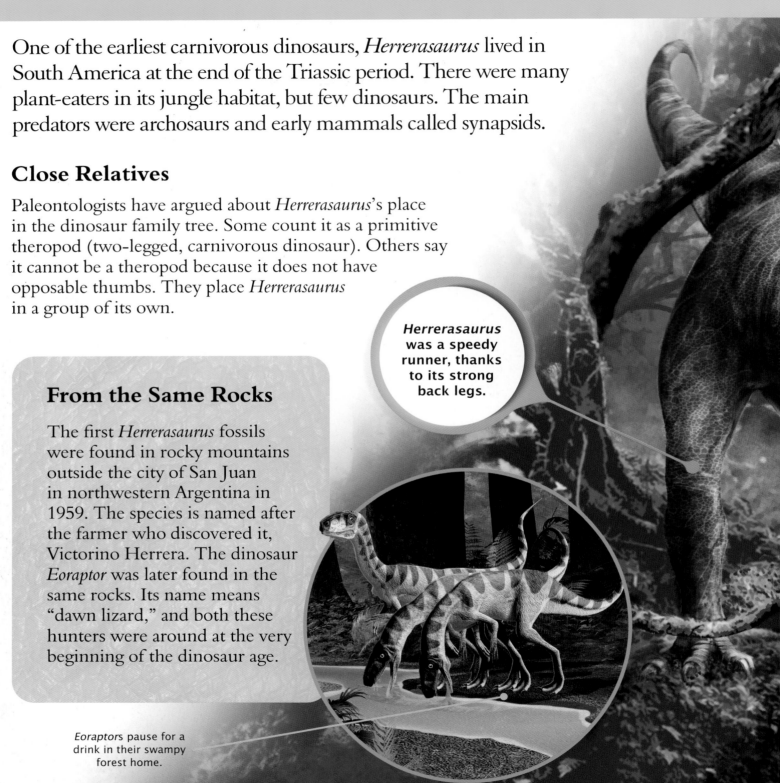

Herrerasaurus

One of the earliest carnivorous dinosaurs, *Herrerasaurus* lived in South America at the end of the Triassic period. There were many plant-eaters in its jungle habitat, but few dinosaurs. The main predators were archosaurs and early mammals called synapsids.

Close Relatives

Paleontologists have argued about *Herrerasaurus*'s place in the dinosaur family tree. Some count it as a primitive theropod (two-legged, carnivorous dinosaur). Others say it cannot be a theropod because it does not have opposable thumbs. They place *Herrerasaurus* in a group of its own.

Herrerasaurus was a speedy runner, thanks to its strong back legs.

From the Same Rocks

The first *Herrerasaurus* fossils were found in rocky mountains outside the city of San Juan in northwestern Argentina in 1959. The species is named after the farmer who discovered it, Victorino Herrera. The dinosaur *Eoraptor* was later found in the same rocks. Its name means "dawn lizard," and both these hunters were around at the very beginning of the dinosaur age.

*Eoraptor*s pause for a drink in their swampy forest home.

DID YOU KNOW? By studying *Herrerasaurus* coprolites (fossils of **dung**!), scientists know that this carnivore crunched up and digested bone.

Experts think *Microraptor* had gleaming, blackish feathers. Like starlings, it was iridescent, appearing different in different lights.

Microraptor hunted small, fast prey including birds.

Microraptor's teeth were serrated on only one side.

Microraptor means "small one who seizes." It used its hand-claws to grip meat or branches.

Deinonychus

The dromaeosaur *Deinonychus* lived in North America during the Early Cretaceous. It probably hunted in packs to bring down prey much larger than itself. Its name means "terrible claw" and its killer weapon was the sickle-shaped claw on its second toe.

Dangerous Family

Dromaeosaurs were formidable hunters. *Deinonychus* was medium-sized, about as large as a wolf. Its cousin *Utahraptor*, also from North America, was one of the largest species. It stood as tall as a person and was around 6 m (20 ft) long.

Working together, a team of *Deinonychus* could kill a juvenile *Tenontosaurus*. An adult was probably too large for them to attack.

In a Flap

Like all dromaeosaurs, *Deinonychus* had feathers. Experts believe that feathers evolved from reptilian scales that had frayed and grown fluffy. They helped dinosaurs to stay warm. In time, feathers were used for display, too. It is possible that *Deinonychus* juveniles could even fly from danger by flapping their arms.

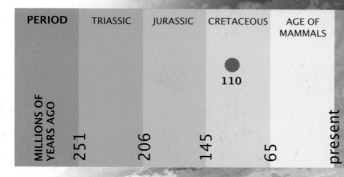

PERIOD	TRIASSIC	JURASSIC	CRETACEOUS	AGE OF MAMMALS

110

| MILLIONS OF YEARS AGO | 251 | 206 | 145 | 65 | present |

Name: *Deinonychus*
(Dye-NON-ik-us)
Family: Dromaeosauridae
Height: 1.2 m (4 ft)
Length: 3.4 m (11.2 ft)
Weight: 85 kg (187 lb)

DINOSAUR PROFILE

Tenontosaurus, the most common plant-eater in its habitat, was often hunted by Deinonychus.

Deinonychus's hooked, second toe was about 13 cm (5 in) long.

Deinonychus's killing method was to stab prey with its claws and then wait for it to bleed to death.

Deinonychus gripped its prey firmly with its claws. A kick could not shake It off.

DID YOU KNOW? *Deinonychus* was first discovered in 1931—but it was not actually given a **name** until 1969.

Spinosaurus

The largest and longest carnivorous dinosaur, *Spinosaurus* lived in North Africa during the Cretaceous. Its pointed, crocodilian snout was perfectly shaped for snapping up fish, but this theropod also fed on dinosaurs and other land animals.

Species and Specimens

Only a handful of fairly complete *Spinosaurus* specimens have been found—and one of those was destroyed in bombing raids on Munich, Germany, during World War II. Most dinosaur experts recognize just one species, which they call *Spinosaurus aegyptiacus* ("Egyptian spine lizard").

Sail or Hump?

Most paleontologists believe that the spines along *Spinosaurus*'s back held up a large sail of skin. A few have another theory—that the spines supported a fatty hump, like a camel's. Either structure could have helped *Spinosaurus* to regulate its temperature, and either could have been used for display, to communicate with other dinosaurs.

Spinosaurus had a series of tall spines sticking out of its backbone. Most experts agree this supported a sail.

PERIOD	TRIASSIC	JURASSIC	CRETACEOUS	AGE OF MAMMALS	present
MILLIONS OF YEARS AGO	251	206	145	65	

105

Name: *Spinosaurus*
(SPY–nuh–SAWR–us)
Family: Spinosauridae
Height: 6 m (20 ft)
Length: 16 m (52.5 ft)
Weight: 9 tonnes (9.9 tons)

DINOSAUR PROFILE

The position of its nostrils suggest that *Spinosaurus* probably spent a lot of its time underwater.

Spinosaurus's narrow skull was up to 1.75 m (5.7 ft) long.

Spinosaurus had short, strong arms.

Primitive fish called coelacanths still exist today—but they are critically endangered.

DID YOU KNOW? The tallest of the **neural spines** along *Spinosaurus*'s back were at least 1.65 m (5.4 ft) long.

Giganotosaurus

When *Giganotosaurus* was discovered in Argentina in 1993, the 12-m- (39-ft-) long carnivore was thought to be the largest theropod in the southern hemisphere—and possibly even the world. Its name means "giant southern lizard."

On the Run

Giganotosaurus is known from preserved tracks as well as fossilized bones. Experts have been able to work out how fast it could run by considering its body size and looking at the spacing between its footprints. Its top speed was probably around 50 km/h (31 mph). By comparison, *Tyrannosaurus rex* (pages 24–25) could reach only 40 km/h (25 mph).

Giganotosaurus

The Carcharodonts

Giganotosaurus was one of the carcharodonts, a group of dinosaurs named after the theropod *Carcharodontosaurus*, which lived in North Africa during the Late Cretaceous. Their sharp, serrated teeth resemble those of the great white shark, *Carcharodon*. Both *Giganotosaurus* and *Carcharodontosaurus* had a gigantic skull with bony ridges overhanging the eyes, massive jaws, and long teeth.

Carcharodontosaurus

PERIOD	TRIASSIC	JURASSIC	CRETACEOUS	AGE OF MAMMALS
			● 98	
MILLIONS OF YEARS AGO	251	206	145	65	present

Name: *Giganotosaurus*
(JIG-an-oh-tuh-SAWR-us)
Family: Carcharodontosauridae
Height: 7 m (23 ft)
Length: 12 m (39 ft)
Weight: 7.3 tonnes (8 tons)

DINOSAUR PROFILE

Giganotosaurus had low, horn–like projections on the bones above and in front of its eyes—just like *Carcharodontosaurus*.

Giganotosaurus had a weaker biting force than *T. rex*, but could snap its jaws shut more quickly.

Giganotosaurus was the apex (top) predator in its habitat.

Giganotosaurus's skull was about 1.8 m (6 ft) long.

Giganotosaurus had powerful, muscular back legs.

DID YOU KNOW? *Giganotosaurus* had a **close cousin**, *Mapusaurus*, which lived in Argentina at the same time and was just as large.

Troodon

Birdlike *Troodon* lived across North America in the Late Cretaceous. Its name means "wounding teeth." When it was first discovered in 1856 it was known from just one fossil, a small and extremely sharp tooth.

Troodon preyed on other dinosaurs, such as young hadrosaurs. It also hunted small mammals and lizards.

Clever Carnivore

Troodon is sometimes described as the most intelligent dinosaur. Compared to other dinosaurs its size, it probably was. Its brain was about six times heavier than theirs. However, it was only as large as an emu's brain today, so *Troodon* cannot have been *that* smart.

Neat Nests

Troodon laid its eggs in bowl-shaped nests over a period of about a week. Just like ostriches today, it is likely that the males and females took turns sitting on the nest to keep the eggs warm. A typical nest contained between 16 and 24 eggs.

Part of a nest of *Troodon* eggs, preserved in rock.

Troodon had binocular vision—forward-pointing eyes that allowed it to judge distances.

Troodon's covering of feathers kept its body warm.

Troodon used its jaws, hands, or feet to grip prey.

PERIOD	TRIASSIC	JURASSIC	CRETACEOUS	AGE OF MAMMALS
MILLIONS OF YEARS AGO	251	206	145	65	present

(77 — Cretaceous)

Name: *Troodon*
(TRO-uh-don)
Family: Troodontidae
Height: 0.9 m (3 ft)
Length: 2.4 m (7.9 ft)
Weight: 50 kg (110 lb)

DINOSAUR PROFILE

DID YOU KNOW? *Troodon*'s relatively **large eyes** let in plenty of light. It could hunt at dawn, at dusk, or even in the middle of the night.

Therizinosaurus

Unlike most other theropods, *Therizinosaurus* was not a meat-eater. Its diet was mostly made up of plants, although it may have also fed on insects and small animals. Its name, meaning "scythe lizard," comes from the three enormous, slashing claws on each hand.

Therizinosaurs

Therizinosaurus has given its name to a group of plant-eating theropods called the therizinosaurs. Others include *Beipiaosaurus*, *Alxasaurus*, and *Erlikosaurus*. As well as their long claws, they were distinguished by their long necks, broad, four-toed feet, and leaf-shaped teeth.

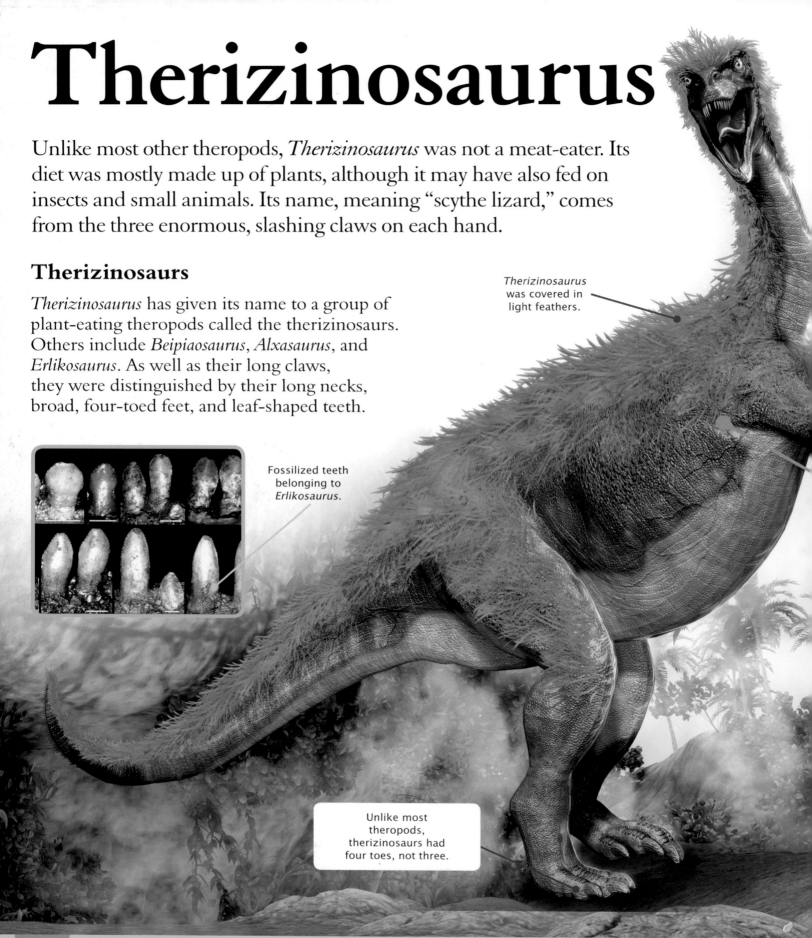

Therizinosaurus was covered in light feathers.

Fossilized teeth belonging to *Erlikosaurus*.

Unlike most theropods, therizinosaurs had four toes, not three.

DID YOU KNOW? Therizinosaurs probably nested in groups. **Seventeen clutches** of eggs were found close to each other in the Gobi Desert, in China, in 2013.

Name: *Therizinosaurus*
(THAIR–uh–zeen–uh–SAWR–us)
Family: Therizinosauridae
Height: 3.7 m (12 ft)
Length: 10 m (33 ft)
Weight: 5 tonnes (5.5 tons)

DINOSAUR PROFILE

Therizinosaurus's
1–m– (3.3–ft–)
long claws could
defend against
predators.

Therizinosaurus
had a bulky body.
It needed a large
stomach for
digesting
plant matter.

Clever Claws

Therizinosaurus lived in what is now
Mongolia at the end of the Cretaceous.
Its claws helped it to fend off predators
such as *Tarbosaurus*, sometimes known
as the Asian *T. rex*. The claws had
other uses, too. Perhaps they cut down
vegetation or allowed the dinosaur to
"fish" for termites in termite mounds.

Being tall enabled
Therizinosaurus
to reach to the
highest branches.

Tyrannosaurus

One species of *Tyrannosaurus* is more famous than any other dinosaur: *Tyrannosaurus rex*, or "king of the tyrant lizards." It inhabited North America at the end of the Cretaceous. For a long time, it was the largest known land carnivore. Today, that title goes to *Spinosaurus* (pages 16–17).

Search for Meat

Tyrannosaurus had binocular vision, which meant that it could locate prey with great accuracy. It could also move fairly quickly, thanks to its muscular back legs. Once it reached its prey, it tore into its flesh with powerful jaws. *Tyrannosaurus*'s teeth could easily crush through bone. Teeth were different sizes, but the longest were around 15 cm (6 in).

One *Tyrannosaurus* sinks its teeth into another's neck.

Life in a Pack

Trackways in Canada show that—at least some of the time—*Tyrannosaurus* hunted in packs. As in wolf packs today, rival males probably fought each other to be pack leader. *Tyrannosaurus* would have used its fearsome jaws not only to kill prey, but to attack rivals.

PERIOD	TRIASSIC	JURASSIC	CRETACEOUS	AGE OF MAMMALS

MILLIONS OF YEARS AGO

251   206   145   65   present

67

Name: *Tyrannosaurus*
(Tye-RAN-uh-SAWR-us)
Family: Tyrannosauridae
Height: 5.5 m (18 ft)
Length: 12 m (39 ft)
Weight: 6.1 tonnes (6.7 tons)

DINOSAUR PROFILE

24

DID YOU KNOW? *Tyrannosaurus*'s 1.2-m- (4-ft-) long jaw contained up to 58 **serrated** teeth.

Tyrannosaurus is estimated to have been able to deliver a stronger bite than any other land animal.

Tyrannosaurus probably had feathers for warmth.

Tail held out behind for balance

Tyrannosaurus walked on slim, birdlike feet. Each foot had three 18–cm– (7–in–) long claws.

Tyrannosaurus's arms were short but powerful. The dinosaur scavenged and hunted.

Melanorosaurus

One of the earliest sauropods, or long-necked plant-eating dinosaurs, *Melanorosaurus* lived between 227 and 208 mya. Its name means "Black Mountain lizard" after the place where it was first discovered: Black Mountain in Transkei, South Africa.

First of the Line

In time, sauropods would become the largest land animals ever. Early species were much smaller—*Melanorosaurus* was just a quarter the length of *Argentinosaurus* (pages 40–41) and far lighter. However, it was still too bulky to walk on two legs and had to lumber along on all fours.

Volcanoes were reshaping the land during the Late Triassic.

All in the Hips

Sauropods (this chapter) belong to the dinosaur group called the saurischians, or lizard-hipped dinosaurs. Their hips were arranged like those of modern lizards. Sauropods were plant-eaters, but the meat-eating theropods (chapter 1) were lizard-hipped, too. The other group of dinosaurs are the ornithischians, or bird-hipped dinosaurs (chapters 3 and 4). They were all plant-eaters.

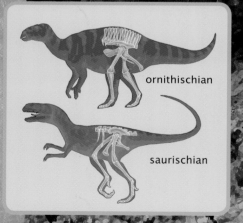

ornithischian

saurischian

Melanorosaurus's long neck allowed it to save energy. It could gather vegetation from a large area without the need to move its whole body.

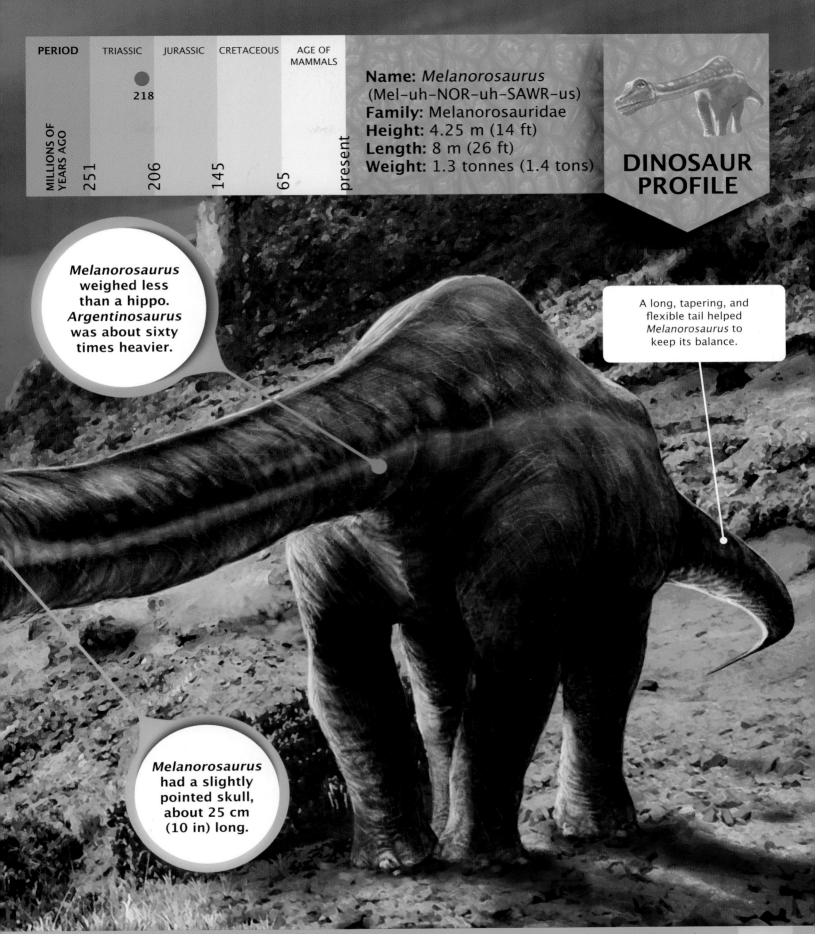

PERIOD	TRIASSIC	JURASSIC	CRETACEOUS	AGE OF MAMMALS
MILLIONS OF YEARS AGO	251	206	145	65	present

218

Name: *Melanorosaurus*
(Mel–uh–NOR–uh–SAWR–us)
Family: Melanorosauridae
Height: 4.25 m (14 ft)
Length: 8 m (26 ft)
Weight: 1.3 tonnes (1.4 tons)

DINOSAUR PROFILE

Melanorosaurus weighed less than a hippo. *Argentinosaurus* was about sixty times heavier.

A long, tapering, and flexible tail helped *Melanorosaurus* to keep its balance.

Melanorosaurus had a slightly pointed skull, about 25 cm (10 in) long.

DID YOU KNOW? Two **close relatives** of *Melanorosaurus* lived in the Late Triassic, too: *Eucnemesaurus*, also from South Africa, and *Riojasaurus* from South America.

Plateosaurus

Since the first fossils were discovered in 1834, *Plateosaurus* has been reconstructed in many ways. It has been shown with its limbs sticking out from its sides like an iguana's and—correctly—with them starting from directly under its body.

Walking the Walk

Experts have also puzzled over whether *Plateosaurus* was quadrupedal (walking on four legs) or bipedal (walking on two). Today, most agree that this European dinosaur was bipedal. Standing on two legs gave it an advantage, because it could reach high in the trees for vegetation.

Plateosaurus's long, narrow jaw had wide, serrated teeth that could shear through tough plant stems.

Compared to other prosauropods, *Plateosaurus* had short arms.

Prosauropods

Plateosaurus belonged to a group called the prosauropods, sauropods' earliest relatives. They walked on two legs, whereas the later, larger sauropods had to walk on four. Some paleontologists think prosauropods also had a more varied diet, and ate some meat as well as plants. *Melanorosaurus* (pages 26–27) used to be classed as prosauropod, too.

DID YOU KNOW? *Plateosaurus* is one of the **best-known** dinosaurs. More than 100 of its skeletons have been found and studied.

PERIOD	TRIASSIC	JURASSIC	CRETACEOUS	AGE OF MAMMALS	present
MILLIONS OF YEARS AGO	251	206	145	65	

209

Name: *Plateosaurus*
(PLAY–tee–uh–SAWR–us)
Family: Plateosauridae
Height: 3 m (9.8 ft)
Length: 7 m (23 ft)
Weight: 1.8 tonnes (2 tons)

DINOSAUR PROFILE

Ten bones, called vertebrae, supported the long, bendy neck.

There were two *Plateosaurus* species. This skull belongs to *Plateosaurus engelhardti*, named after Johann Engelhardt, the German doctor who discovered it.

Plateosaurus grips a branch with its clawed hands.

Mamenchisaurus

Mamenchisaurus lived in what is now China between 160 and 145 mya. So far, seven species have been discovered. They vary greatly in size but all share one characteristic—an extra-long neck that makes up around half of their total body length.

Great and Small

The first *Mamenchisaurus* fossils, found in the 1950s, belonged to a species called *Mamenchisaurus constructus* (the *constructus* part of the name came from it being discovered on a building site). The record-breaker of the family was named in the 1990s. Known as *Mamenchisaurus sinocanadorum*, it was three times as long, with a body length of 35 m (115 ft) and an 18-m (59-ft) neck.

Hunters such as *Yangchuanosaurus* had to team up to bring down a *Mamenchisaurus*.

Mamenchisaurus's main predator was an allosaur called *Yangchuanosaurus*.

PERIOD	TRIASSIC	JURASSIC	CRETACEOUS	AGE OF MAMMALS
MILLIONS OF YEARS AGO	251	206	145	65	present

153

Name: *Mamenchisaurus* (Mah–MEN–chih–SAWR–us)
Family: Mamenchisauridae
Height: 12 m (40 ft)
Length: 35 m (115 ft)
Weight: 12 tonnes (13 tons)

DINOSAUR PROFILE

DID YOU KNOW? One species of *Mamenchisaurus* is thought to have had a defensive **tail club**.

Reaching Out

Mamenchisaurus's long neck could have reached up high, but most experts believe that this dinosaur fed mostly on low-lying vegetation. Having a long neck was still an advantage. *Mamenchisaurus* could reach out for food across a large area without having to use up energy moving its body from place to place.

No one can be sure what noises sauropods made.

Mamenchisaurus could rear up to frighten off predators.

A small group of *Mamenchisaurus* go to the river to drink. Like all sauropods, this dinosaur lived in herds.

Brachiosaurus

When it was discovered in 1903, *Brachiosaurus* was the largest known dinosaur. Paleontologists did not believe that such an enormous animal could have supported its own weight on land. They thought that it must have lived in water.

Nose Knowhow

In early reconstructions, *Brachiosaurus*'s nostrils were located on a bump between its eyes, where they could be used to breathe even when the rest of the head was submerged. Today, paleontologists know *Brachiosaurus* lived on land, not water, and position the nostrils further down the snout. The nostrils were relatively large, so the dinosaur probably had a good sense of smell.

Brachiosaurus had 58 leaf-shaped teeth for stripping plants of shoots, leaves, and cones.

Eating Machines

Just like today's large herbivores, sauropods moved in herds, constantly eating and seeking out new feeding grounds. Experts estimate that *Brachiosaurus* consumed 120 kg (264 lb) of vegetation a day. Despite this, it shared its environment with other plant-eating giants, including *Apatosaurus* and *Diplodocus*.

PERIOD	TRIASSIC	JURASSIC	CRETACEOUS	AGE OF MAMMALS
MILLIONS OF YEARS AGO	251	206	145 ● 152	65 present

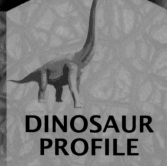

Name: *Brachiosaurus* (BRACK-ee-uh-SAWR-us)
Family: Brachiosauridae
Height: 9 m (30 ft)
Length: 30 m (98 ft)
Weight: 70 tonnes (77 tons)

DINOSAUR PROFILE

Unlike other sauropods, *Brachiosaurus* had longer front legs than back ones. Its back sloped down toward the tail.

Brachiosaurus held its neck upright, like a giraffe. One early species has since been renamed *Giraffatitan*.

Brachiosaurus lived in Late Jurassic North America.

Brachiosaurus's huge bulk helped it to conserve its body heat.

DID YOU KNOW? *Brachiosaurus* means **"arm lizard."** The name comes from it having longer front legs, or arms.

Amargasaurus

One of the smallest sauropods, 10-m- (33-ft-) long *Amargasaurus* lived around 125 mya in what is now Argentina. The sharp spines along its neck and back might have been to defend against predators or for showing off to rivals or mates.

Double Find

Amargasaurus was found on an expedition led by the Argentinian paleontologist José Bonaparte. The team discovered an almost complete skeleton. They found another dinosaur on that trip: the Late Cretaceous predator *Carnotaurus*. Like *Amargasaurus*, it is known from only one skeleton.

One theory is that *Amargasaurus*'s spines supported sails of skin that helped to keep its temperature steady.

The one *Amargasaurus* skeleton was discovered in 1984.

Feeding Strategy

Amargasaurus is one of the dicraosaurids. The family is named after *Dicraeosaurus*, a small sauropod of Late Jurassic Tanzania, eastern Africa. Being smaller than other sauropods meant that dicraeosaurids did not have to compete for plants. They were browsing for vegetation at a different level.

Amargasaurus's broad snout was lined with long, cylinder–shaped teeth.

DID YOU KNOW? *Amargasaurus* was found at a place in Argentina called **La Amarga Arroyo**. Its name means "lizard from La Amarga."

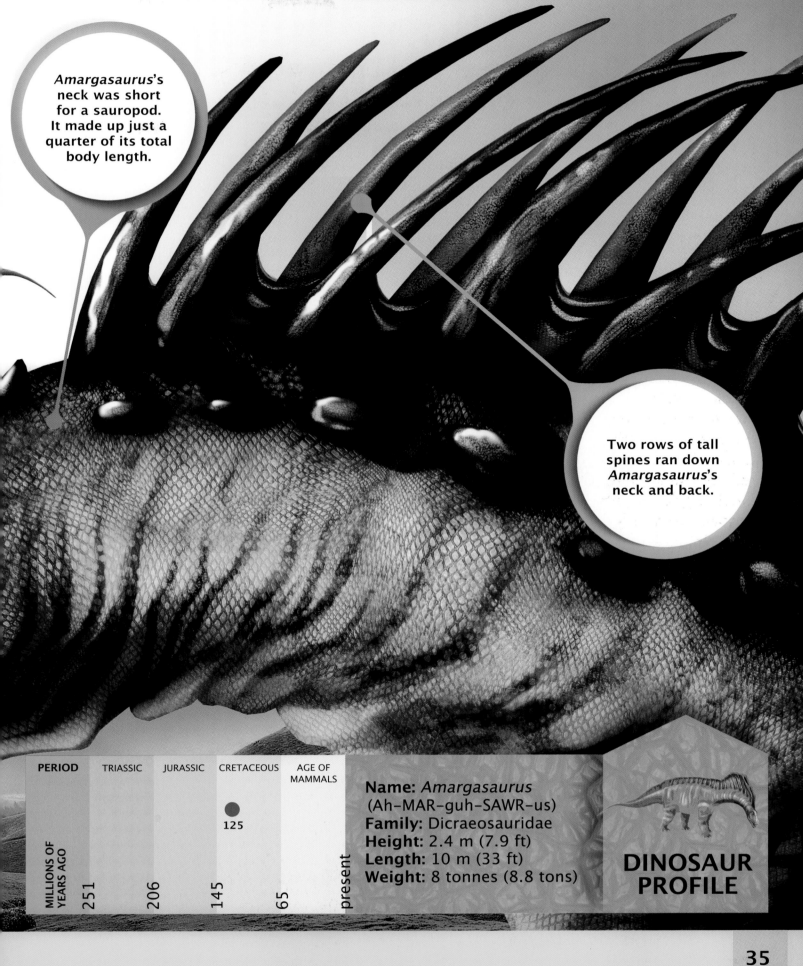

Amargasaurus's neck was short for a sauropod. It made up just a quarter of its total body length.

Two rows of tall spines ran down *Amargasaurus*'s neck and back.

PERIOD	TRIASSIC	JURASSIC	CRETACEOUS	AGE OF MAMMALS

125

MILLIONS OF YEARS AGO

251

206

145

65

present

Name: *Amargasaurus*
(Ah–MAR–guh–SAWR–us)
Family: Dicraeosauridae
Height: 2.4 m (7.9 ft)
Length: 10 m (33 ft)
Weight: 8 tonnes (8.8 tons)

DINOSAUR PROFILE

Nigersaurus

Named after the West African country where it had been discovered in the 1970s, *Nigersaurus* was an unusual, elephant-sized sauropod. Its fossilized remains were found in the Sahara Desert, but in the Early Cretaceous this landscape was a great floodplain with rivers and lush vegetation.

Tooth Talk

Nigersaurus's straight-edged snout was packed with more than 500 teeth for munching on low-growing plants. At least 50 tiny teeth lined the front of its mouth—with about eight rows of replacement teeth behind them, ready and waiting. Cutting through fibrous vegetation was a tough job. Each tooth lasted only a couple of weeks.

Having teeth at the front of the muzzle allowed *Nigersaurus* to "mow" plants close to the ground.

PERIOD	TRIASSIC	JURASSIC	CRETACEOUS	AGE OF MAMMALS
MILLIONS OF YEARS AGO	251	206	145 · 110 · 65	present

Name: *Nigersaurus* (NI–juh–SAWR–us)
Family: Rebbachisauridae
Height: 1.9 m (6.2 ft)
Length: 9 m (30 ft)
Weight: 4 tonnes (4.4 tons)

DINOSAUR PROFILE

DID YOU KNOW? The **smallest** *Nigersaurus* fossil is a jawbone that belonged to a tiny hatchling. It is less than 2.5 cm (1 in) across.

Fellow Fossils

Nigersaurus was found in the Elrhaz Formation, a band of Early Cretaceous rock in Niger, Central Africa. Other dinosaurs discovered there include the fish-eating spinosaur *Suchomimus* and the hadrosaur *Ouranosaurus*. The super-crocodile *Sarcosuchus* is also known from the Elrhaz Formation.

Nigersaurus kept its head close to the ground, raising it only to look for predators.

Nigersaurus's snout broadened out at the end.

Nigersaurus had huge eyes for a sauropod, but its nostrils were small. It probably had a poor sense of smell.

Nigersaurus fed on mosses, ferns, and horsetails.

Sauroposeidon

In 1994, a few fossilized neck bones were discovered by a dog walker in Oklahoma, U.S.A. They belonged to *Sauroposeidon*. At 18 m (59 ft) high, it was the tallest known dinosaur, and almost as heavy as *Argentinosaurus* (pages 40–41).

Hot and Humid

Herbivorous *Sauroposeidon* lived around the shores of what is now the Gulf of Mexico 110 mya. At that time, the landscape was made up of rainforests, river deltas, and wetlands. The climate was tropical (hot and humid all year round) or subtropical (with hot, wet summers and short, mild winters).

Swampy Habitat

Sauroposeidon was named after Poseidon—the Greek god of earthquakes as well as the sea—because its huge bulk would have made the ground shake. *Sauroposeidon* was the only large sauropod around at that time. The top predator was *Acrocanthosaurus*, which preyed on young *Sauroposeidon* whenever it had the opportunity.

Fossilized *Sauroposeidon* footprints have been found in Texas, U.S.A.

Like other sauropods, *Sauroposeidon* lived in herds.

PERIOD	TRIASSIC	JURASSIC	CRETACEOUS	AGE OF MAMMALS	present
MILLIONS OF YEARS AGO	251	206	145	65	

110

Name: *Sauroposeidon*
(SAWR–oh–puh–SIGH–don)
Family: Titanosauridae
Height: 18 m (59 ft)
Length: 34 m (112 ft)
Weight: 55 tonnes (60 tons)

DINOSAUR PROFILE

The estimated neck length was 12 m (39 ft). The largest bone, or vertebra, was a record–breaking 1.2 m (4 ft) long.

Vegetation included palms, tree ferns, and magnolias.

Sauroposeidon juveniles may have lived with the herd for protection.

DID YOU KNOW? *Sauroposeidon* may have had a close cousin. Giant vertebrae were discovered in England, UK, in 2004.

39

Argentinosaurus

The area that is now South America was warm and wet at the end of the Cretaceous, and home to some enormous, plant-eating dinosaurs. *Argentinosaurus* ("Argentina lizard") was one of the largest animals to have ever lived on land. Each of its vertebrae (spine bones) was almost as tall as a person.

Its long neck allowed the dinosaur to reach for food without moving much.

This unnamed titanosaur was even bigger than *Argentinosaurus*—as tall as a seven-storey building!

Record-Breakers

A farmer found the first *Argentinosaurus* fossil by accident in 1987. At first, he mistook the massive leg bone for a petrified tree trunk. *Argentinosaurus* was a record-breaker for more than two decades, until a new species of titanosaur was discovered. Still unnamed, it was 40 m (131 ft) long, 20 m (66 ft) tall, and weighed 77 tonnes (85 tons).

PERIOD	TRIASSIC	JURASSIC	CRETACEOUS	AGE OF MAMMALS
MILLIONS OF YEARS AGO	251	206	145	65 / present

95

Name: *Argentinosaurus* (AH-gen-teen-uh-SAWR-us)
Family: Antarctosauridae
Height: 7.3 m (24 ft)
Length: 35 m (115 ft)
Weight: 73 tonnes (80 tons)

DINOSAUR PROFILE

DID YOU KNOW? *Argentinosaurus* eggs were about the size of **rugby balls**.

Titanosaur Teeth

Argentinosaurus belonged to the group of sauropods called the titanosaurs that flourished after the large Jurassic sauropods had died out. Their nostrils were set high on the snout, and they had a jaw packed with peg-like teeth.

Argentinosaurus probably couldn"t raise its neck much above shoulder height.

The long tail stuck out behind for balance.

Argentinosaurus may have taken 40 years to reach its adult size.

Thick, sturdy legs supported its heavy bulk.

Saltasaurus

Herds of the titanosaur *Saltasaurus* lived in Argentina at the end of the Cretaceous. When this dinosaur was discovered, it was the first sauropod known to have bony bumps, called osteoderms, on its skin. These may have helped to protect *Saltasaurus*, which was relatively small for a sauropod.

Saltasaurus had small feet and short, stubby legs.

Titanosaur Nursery

A *Saltasaurus* nesting site was discovered in Argentina in 1997. The dinosaurs had used it for hundreds of years. Most of the time, the female *Saltasaurus* laid their eggs, the eggs hatched, and the youngsters left the site. However, the site was on a floodplain. Every so often the river flooded and eggs were buried in the mud and fossilized.

Saltasaurus did not guard its nest, but may have covered it with earth or plants to keep the eggs warm and hidden from predators.

PERIOD	TRIASSIC	JURASSIC	CRETACEOUS	AGE OF MAMMALS
MILLIONS OF YEARS AGO	251	206	145	65 · present

70

Name: *Saltasaurus* (Salt-uh-SAWR-us)
Family: Saltasauridae
Height: 5 m (16.4 ft)
Length: 12 m (40 ft)
Weight: 7 tonnes (7.7 tons)

DINOSAUR PROFILE

Saltasaurus's head was supported on a small neck. The tail was short, too.

Skin Story

Saltasaurus's species name, *loricatus*, means "protected by plates." Its skin had osteoderms in two sizes. The larger ones were 12 cm (4.7 in) long and oval. Between these were small, round ones, just 0.7 cm (0.3 in) across. Paleontologists now know of other sauropods with osteoderms, such as 18-m- (60-ft-) long *Laplatasaurus*, also from Late Cretaceous Argentina.

There is only one known species of *Saltasaurus*: *Saltasaurus loricatus*.

Saltasaurus ate around 205 kg (452 lb) of plant matter a day.

DID YOU KNOW? A *Saltasaurus* egg was just 12 cm (4.7 in) across—not even as large as an **ostrich** egg.

Rapetosaurus

Many titanosaurs are known from only a few bones, but *Rapetosaurus*'s fossils included a nearly complete skeleton. This dinosaur lived 70 mya on the island of Madagascar, off the east coast of Africa.

Stomach Stones

Like all sauropods, *Rapetosaurus* did not chew its food properly. Instead, it swallowed stones called gastroliths to grind up the plant food in its stomach.

These gastroliths were smoothed and polished inside a dinosaur's stomach.

Rapetosaurus had bony bumps, called osteoderms, on its skin.

Juvenile Joker

Rapetosaurus was discovered by American paleontologist Kristina Curry Rogers. She named it after Rapeto, a giant trickster in Madagascan mythology. The skeleton Rogers found and studied was 8 m (26 ft) long from nose to tail and belonged to a juvenile. Adult *Rapetosaurus* grew to 15 m (50 ft).

Rapetosaurus swallowed stones to help mash and bash vegetation in its gut.

Rapetosaurus was the first titanosaur found with its skull still attached to the rest of its skeleton.

Rapetosaurus needed a huge heart and lungs.

PERIOD	TRIASSIC	JURASSIC	CRETACEOUS	AGE OF MAMMALS

MILLIONS OF YEARS AGO

251   206   145   65   present

68

Name: *Rapetosaurus*
(Ruh–PAY–tuh–SAWR–us)
Family: Nemegtosauridae
Height: 5.5 m (18 ft)
Length: 15 m (50 ft)
Weight: 22.5 tonnes (25 tons)

DINOSAUR PROFILE

DID YOU KNOW? One *Rapetosaurus* fossil is of a baby that probably **starved** to death when it was just a month or two old. It would have weighed around 40 kg (88 lb).

Heterodontosaurus

One of the earliest ornithischians, or bird-hipped dinosaurs (page 26), *Heterodontosaurus* lived in South Africa about 195 mya. Its name means "different toothed lizard." Unlike most reptiles, it had teeth of several different shapes.

Tooth Types

Heterodontosaurus's square cheek teeth were used for grinding and chewing. At the front of its beak-like, horny snout, it had smaller front teeth for snipping off plant stems. Finally, it had a pair of curved tusks.

Heterodontosaurus probably used its tusks to show off to rivals.

Discoveries

The first *Heterodontosaurus* fossil was a skull, discovered in 1961. Five years later another skull was found—this time attached to an almost perfect skeleton. Since then, more finds have surfaced. The most complete skeleton was in 2005 but it could not be excavated because it had fossilized in such hard rock.

A cast of the *Heterodontosaurus* skeleton discovered in 1966.

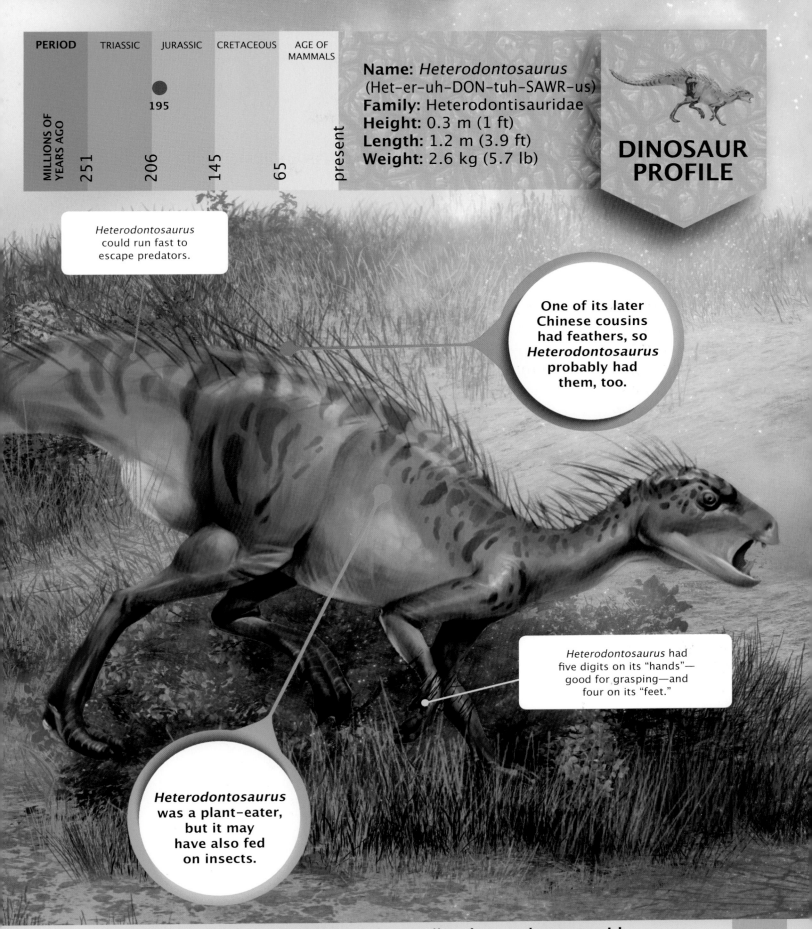

PERIOD	TRIASSIC	JURASSIC	CRETACEOUS	AGE OF MAMMALS	
MILLIONS OF YEARS AGO	251	206	145	65	present

195

Name: *Heterodontosaurus*
(Het–er–uh–DON–tuh–SAWR–us)
Family: Heterodontisauridae
Height: 0.3 m (1 ft)
Length: 1.2 m (3.9 ft)
Weight: 2.6 kg (5.7 lb)

DINOSAUR PROFILE

Heterodontosaurus could run fast to escape predators.

One of its later Chinese cousins had feathers, so *Heterodontosaurus* probably had them, too.

Heterodontosaurus had five digits on its "hands"— good for grasping—and four on its "feet."

Heterodontosaurus was a plant-eater, but it may have also fed on insects.

DID YOU KNOW? *Fruitadens* was the smallest **heterodontosaurid**.
It was just 70 cm (27.5 in) long and lived in Late Jurassic North America.

Hypsilophodon

During the Early Cretaceous, the Isle of Wight, a small island off the south coast of England, was home to a small, fast-moving dinosaur called *Hypsilophodon*. It browsed on tough plants such as ferns and cycads and probably lived in herds for safety.

Threatening Theropods

The main hunters in *Hypsilophodon*'s habitat were *Baryonyx*, *Eotyrannus*, and *Neovenator*. *Baryonyx* had a narrow jaw and was probably a specialist fish eater. *Eotyrannus* was a pony-sized tyrannosaur. The top predator was a 7.6-m- (25-ft-) long allosaur called *Neovenator* ("new hunter").

Hypsilophodon's short, beak-like snout was ideal for snapping off low-growing plants.

The landscape was hot and usually dry. Any rain caused flash floods.

PERIOD	TRIASSIC	JURASSIC	CRETACEOUS	AGE OF MAMMALS	present
MILLIONS OF YEARS AGO	251	206	145	65	

128

Name: *Hypsilophodon*
(Hip-sih-LO-fuh-don)
Family: Hypsilophodontidae
Height: 0.6 m (2 ft)
Length: 1.8 m (5.9 ft)
Weight: 20 kg (44 lb)

DINOSAUR PROFILE

DID YOU KNOW? More than 100 *Hypsilophodon* skeletons have been found on one Isle of Wight beach, **Brighstone Bay**.

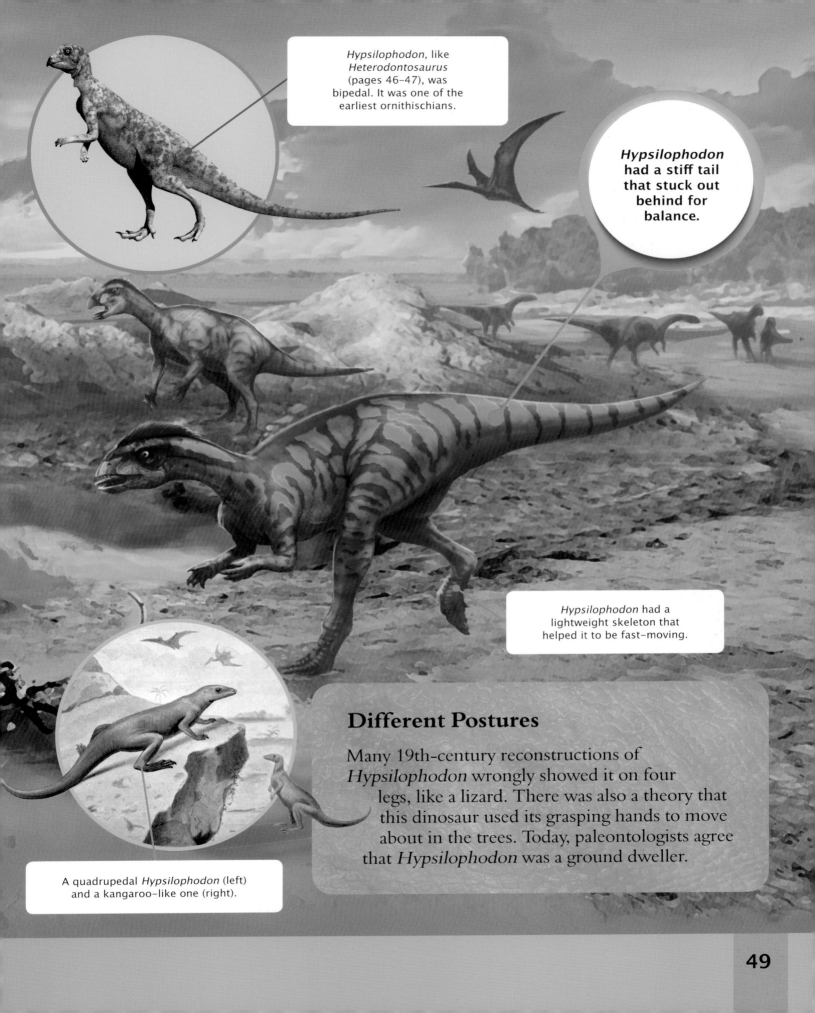

Hypsilophodon, like *Heterodontosaurus* (pages 46–47), was bipedal. It was one of the earliest ornithischians.

Hypsilophodon had a stiff tail that stuck out behind for balance.

Hypsilophodon had a lightweight skeleton that helped it to be fast-moving.

Different Postures

Many 19th-century reconstructions of *Hypsilophodon* wrongly showed it on four legs, like a lizard. There was also a theory that this dinosaur used its grasping hands to move about in the trees. Today, paleontologists agree that *Hypsilophodon* was a ground dweller.

A quadrupedal *Hypsilophodon* (left) and a kangaroo-like one (right).

Iguanodon

The large plant-eater *Iguanodon* roamed across Europe and North America during the Early and Mid Cretaceous. More than 25 species are known. *Iguanodon* moved in herds for protection against predators such as *Deinonychus* (pages 14–15).

Iguanodon walked on all fours, with its body and tail parallel to the ground.

Some experts think that *Iguanodon* may have had cheek pouches for storing food.

Iguanodon sometimes reared up to reach for food or look for danger.

DID YOU KNOW? English geologist Gideon Mantell named *Iguanodon* in 1825— 17 years before paleontologist **Richard Owen** coined the word "dinosaur."

Eating Technique

Iguanodon had a toothless beak for cropping off tough horsetails and ferns, and wide cheek teeth for mashing and pulping plant matter. The teeth were similar to a modern-day iguana's (*Iguanodon* means "iguana tooth").

Iguanodon's tail stuck out stiffly behind it.

Early Finds

Iguanodon was only the second dinosaur to be named (the first was *Megalosaurus*). The first fossils were a few teeth from southern England. The most spectacular finds came from a coal mine at Bernissart in Belgium. Nearly 40 *Iguanodon* skeletons were uncovered there in 1878.

Iguanodon had a vicious thumb spike to stab at would-be attackers.

An *Iguanodon* skeleton from Bernissart, Belgium, being mounted for display

PERIOD	TRIASSIC	JURASSIC	CRETACEOUS	AGE OF MAMMALS	present
MILLIONS OF YEARS AGO	251	206	145	65	

121

Name: *Iguanodon*
(Ig-WAN-oh-don)
Family: Iguanodontidae
Height: 3.25 m (10.7 ft)
Length: 10 m (33 ft)
Weight: 3.1 tonnes (3.4 tons)

DINOSAUR PROFILE

Leaellynasaura

Large-eyed *Leaellynasaura* lived about 110 mya. During the winter months this plant-eater had to cope with total darkness and cooler temperatures because its forest habitat lay inside the Antarctic Circle.

The Antarctic Circle was warmer in the Cretaceous than it is today.

Like all hypsilophodonts, *Leaellynasaura* was small and speedy. It moved around on two legs.

Leaellynasaura relied on its excellent eyesight to look out for predators.

Leaellynasaura's long tail contained more than 70 vertebrae.

Name: *Leaellynasaura*
(Lee–ELL–in–ah–SAWR–ah)
Family: Hypsilophontidae
Height: 0.6 m (2 ft)
Length: 1.8 m (5.9 ft)
Weight: 20 kg (44 lb)

DINOSAUR PROFILE

Dinosaur Cove

Leaellynasaura was discovered in 1989 at Dinosaur Cove in Victoria, on the coast of southeast Australia. The sand- and mudstone cliffs there formed in the Early Cretaceous. Other dinosaurs found at the site include another two-legged plant-eater, *Atlascopcosaurus*, and a small theropod called *Timimus*.

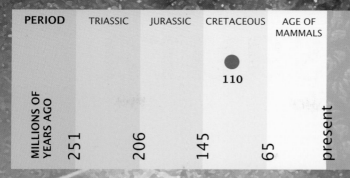

This image of *Leaellynasaura* was created for an Australian postage stamp.

In the Early Cretaceous, Dinosaur Cove was a floodplain. There were conifers, gingkos, and monkey puzzle trees.

Keeping Warm

During the Early Cretaceous, the southern tip of Australia fell within the Antarctic Circle. Temperatures were milder than they are today. However, there still would have been less food during the long winter months when that part of the Earth was facing away from the Sun. There is no evidence that *Leaellynasaura* hibernated, but it may have sheltered in burrows.

DID YOU KNOW? The paleontologists who discovered *Leaellynasaura*, Thomas Rich and Patricia Vickers–Rich, named it after their daughter, **Leaellyn**.

Gasparinisaura

Speedy little plant-eater *Gasparinisaura* lived in Argentina around 85 mya. It belonged to the same family as much larger *Iguanodon* (pages 50–51) and fed on tough vegetation, including conifers and cycads.

Daily Grind

Stones called gastroliths (page 44) have been found with *Gasparinisaura*. Its stomach could contain as many as 140 stones, each less than 1 cm (0.4 in) across. Plant matter was ground up as it passed between the stones, making it easier to digest.

Tiny *Gasparinisaura* skeletons on display in Copenhagen, Denmark.

Large eyes, high on its head, gave *Gasparinisaura* good all-round vision, so that it could spot danger.

PERIOD	TRIASSIC	JURASSIC	CRETACEOUS	AGE OF MAMMALS	
MILLIONS OF YEARS AGO	251	206	145	65	present

85

Name: *Gasparinisaura* (Gas-pah-reen-ee-SAWR-uh)
Family: Iguanodontidae
Height: 0.8 m (2.6 ft)
Length: 1.7 m (5.6 ft)
Weight: 13 kg (6.6 lb)

DINOSAUR PROFILE

DID YOU KNOW? *Gasparinisaura* was named after the Argentinian paleontologist Zulma Brandoni de **Gasparini**. Two members of her team discovered the dinosaur.

Living with Giants

Gasparinisaura fossils come from rock that formed in what is now Patagonia, Argentina, during the Late Cretaceous. Other species found nearby include the titanosaurs *Argentinosaurus* (pages 40–41), *Saltasaurus* (pages 42–43), and *Antarctosaurus*, and the theropods *Aucasaurus* and *Abelisaurus*.

Gasparinisaura shared its habitat with some of the largest ever sauropods, *Argentinosaurus*.

Gasparinisaura probably had a thumb spike like its cousin, *Iguanodon*.

Parasaurolophus

One of the hadrosaurs, or duck-billed dinosaurs, herbivorous *Parasaurolophus* lived across North America around 75 mya. It was thought to be a close relative of another hadrosaur, *Saurolophus* ("crested lizard"). *Parasaurolophus* means "like *Saurolophus*."

Skull Features

In fact, *Saurolophus*'s crest was mostly solid, while *Parasaurolophus*'s was hollow. It had tubes leading to and from the nostrils and amplified the dinosaur's calls (made them louder). *Parasaurolophus*'s closest relative was the large Asian hadrosaur *Charonosaurus*.

The crest made its calls travel further.

Parasaurolophus went up on two legs to run or look out for danger.

Parasaurolophus's short, stout legs helped it to push through thick undergrowth.

Parasaurolophus grazed on all fours.

Hot Head

Some paleontologists believe that *Parasaurolophus*'s crest helped it to keep its body temperature steady. It could have soaked up heat during the daytime to keep *Parasaurolophus* warm at night. Another possibility is that *Parasaurolophus* could lose excess body heat through its crest, to stop it becoming too hot.

Including the crest, *Parasaurolophus*'s skull could be more than 2 m (6.6 ft) long, depending on the species.

Parasaurolophus communicated with members of the herd to warn of predators or to attract a mate.

The crest grew larger with age. It may have looked different in males and females.

PERIOD	TRIASSIC	JURASSIC	CRETACEOUS	AGE OF MAMMALS
MILLIONS OF YEARS AGO	251	206	145	65

75

present

Name: *Parasaurolophus* (Par-ah-SAWR-OL-uh-fus)
Family: Hadrosauridae
Height: 3.6 m (12 ft)
Length: 11 m (36 ft)
Weight: 2.5 tonnes (2.8 tons)

DINOSAUR PROFILE

DID YOU KNOW? At least three species of *Parasaurolophus* have been identified. The first, *Parasaurolophus walkeri*, was discovered as long ago as **1920**.

Lambeosaurus

All the hollow-crested hadrosaurs are known as the lambeosaurines, after *Lambeosaurus*. Like *Parasaurolophus* (pages 56–57) *Lambeosaurus* lived in North America around 75 mya. It was named after Lawrence Lambe, the Canadian paleontologist who first studied it.

Dinosaur Park Formation

The layer of rock in Alberta, Canada, where *Lambeosaurus* was discovered is called the Dinosaur Park Formation. It contains other hadrosaurs, including *Parasaurolophus* and *Corythosaurus*, pachycephalosaurs such as *Stegoceras* (pages 72–73), ceratopsians including *Styracosaurus* (pages 74–75), and ankylosaurs such as *Edmontonia* (pages 100–101) and *Euoplocephalus* (pages 102–103).

The crest looked like an axehead.

Lambeosaurus had more than 100 teeth in its cheeks for chewing.

The American paleontologist Barnum Brown excavated the first *Corythosaurus* specimen in 1912.

Complicated Cousin

Corythosaurus, whose name means "helmeted lizard," was the same size as *Lambeosaurus* and lived in the same habitat. The main difference was the complex passages inside its crest. These would have turned any calls *Corythosaurus* made into very deep, low-pitched sounds that could travel great distances.

PERIOD	TRIASSIC	JURASSIC	CRETACEOUS	AGE OF MAMMALS

MILLIONS OF YEARS AGO

251   206   145   75   65   present

Name: *Lambeosaurus*
(LAM-be-uh-SAWR-us)
Family: Hadrosauridae
Height: 4 m (13 ft)
Length: 10 m (32 ft)
Weight: 4.5 tonnes (5 tons)

The crest may have been used for display, to amplify sounds, and perhaps even to improve *Lambeosaurus*'s sense of smell.

The plant-eater lived in swampy forests.

Lambeosaurus moved around on four legs or two, so it could reach plants growing at different levels.

DID YOU KNOW? In the past, some paleontologists argued that *Lambeosaurus* was **aquatic** and that its crest acted as a snorkel!

59

Shantungosaurus

Not all duck-billed dinosaurs had a crest. *Shantungosaurus*, one of the largest known hadrosaurs, did not have one. It may have had its own method of making its calls distinctive—an inflatable flap of skin near its nostrils that made sounds.

From Shandong

Shantungosaurus means "Shandong lizard," after the province of eastern China where the dinosaur was discovered. It was named in 1973 and five incomplete skeletons have been dug up to date. When *Shantungosaurus* was alive, the environment was a humid floodplain.

Shantungosaurus has knocked over a predatory *Tarbosaurus* with a powerful swipe of its tail.

DID YOU KNOW? *Shantungosaurus*'s **femur** (thighbone) was 1.7 m (5.6 ft) long.

PERIOD	TRIASSIC	JURASSIC	CRETACEOUS	AGE OF MAMMALS	
MILLIONS OF YEARS AGO	251	206	145	74 • 65	present

Name: *Shantungosaurus*
(Shan–TUNG–o–SAWR–us)
Family: Hadrosauridae
Height: 5 m (16.4 ft)
Length: 15.5 m (51 ft)
Weight: 16 tonnes (18 tons)

DINOSAUR PROFILE

The 1.6-m
(5.3-ft) skull ended
with a toothless
beak. The jaws
contained
1,500 tiny teeth.

Good Mothers

One of the best-known duck-bills
is *Maiasaura*, whose name means
"good mother lizard." *Maiasaura*
nurseries have been uncovered and
experts believe that this dinosaur
incubated its eggs and may even
have cared for its young. Perhaps
other hadrosaurs also did this.

Shantungosaurus
hatchlings may
have been too
helpless to
find food for
themselves.

Hadrosaurs laid
round eggs.

Edmontosaurus

One of the largest hadrosaurs, *Edmontosaurus* lived at the end of the dinosaur age. It was the North American cousin of Asian *Shantungosaurus* (pages 60–61). It was named after Edmonton, capital city of Alberta, the Canadian province where *Edmontosaurus* was found.

Walking and Running

Usually, herbivorous *Edmontosaurus* walked on all fours. It could run at speeds faster than 50 km/h (31 mph), typically on two legs but sometimes on four. Running was its best way to escape predators. One *Edmontosaurus* was found with a theropod bite on its tail bone.

Edmontosaurus had a small crest, or comb. It was made of skin and scales, not bone.

Edmontosaurus's backbone was held horizontally above the hip bone.

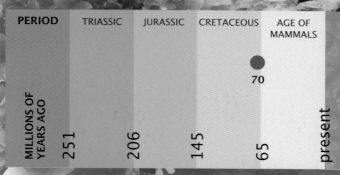

PERIOD	TRIASSIC	JURASSIC	CRETACEOUS	AGE OF MAMMALS		present
MILLIONS OF YEARS AGO	251	206	145	70 65		

Name: *Edmontosaurus*
(Ed–MON–tuh–SAWR–us)
Family: Hadrosauridae
Height: 3.5 m (11.5 ft)
Length: 12 m (39 ft)
Weight: 4 tonnes (4.4 tons)

DINOSAUR PROFILE

The long, narrow skull ended in a beaky mouth.

Paleontologists have been able to study fossilized *Edmontosaurus* skin.

No Limits

Some experts think that *Edmontosaurus* could have grown as large as *Shantungosaurus*—if an individual managed to live long enough. Their evidence is a 7.6-m (25-ft) *Edmontosaurus* tail. Unfortunately most *Edmontosaurus* seem to have died before reaching that size, because of predators, disease, or some other disaster.

As *Edmontosaurus* grew older, its skull became longer and flatter.

DID YOU KNOW? Many species of *Edmontosaurus* have been identified over the years. At the moment, **just two** are officially recognized.

Thescelosaurus

The first *Thescelosaurus* fossil was found in 1891, but then stored in a crate and ignored for more than 20 years. When it was finally studied, it was named *Thescelosaurus neglectus* (*Thescelosaurus* means "wonderful lizard" and *neglectus* means "ignored").

Willo's Heart of Stone

In 2000 experts in North Carolina, U.S.A., introduced the most complete *Thescelosaurus* skeleton. They called it Willo and claimed it had a heart. Fossilized hearts are extremely rare because they are made up of soft tissue. Unfortunately, experts now think the "heart" is just a lump of rock that formed during fossilization.

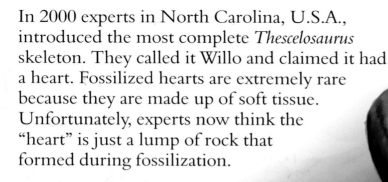

Thescelosaurus's thighs were longer than its calves. (Fast-running ornithopods had the opposite—longer calves and shorter thighs.)

Paleontologists thought this dark ring inside Willo's chest might be its heart.

PERIOD	TRIASSIC	JURASSIC	CRETACEOUS	AGE OF MAMMALS	
MILLIONS OF YEARS AGO	251	206	145	65	present

66

Name: *Thescelosaurus*
(Theh-SEL-uh-SAWR-us)
Family: Thescelosauridae
Height: 1.75 m (5.7 ft)
Length: 3.75 m (12.3 ft)
Weight: 250 kg (550 lb)

DINOSAUR PROFILE

Just Plants?

Thescelosaurus has been found across North America, from Canada to New Mexico. It lived on floodplains, along riverbanks, and beside lakes. It had the leaf-shaped teeth at the back of its mouth that most herbivores have. However, it also had short, pointy front teeth, which might mean that it also ate some meat.

This *Thescelosaurus* skeleton came from the Hell Creek Formation in Montana, U.S.A.

Thescelosaurus's small front teeth suggest that it might have been an omnivore.

Thescelosaurus ran upright on two legs.

DID YOU KNOW? The *Thescelosaurus* Willo contains organic, **cell−like material**. It could be from plants that it ate—or it could be from Willo itself.

Yinlong

The best-known of the ceratopsians (dinosaurs with horned faces) is *Triceratops* (pages 82–83), who lived during the Late Cretaceous. However, the first dinosaurs in this group appeared much earlier. *Yinlong* is the oldest, most primitive ceratopsian that is known.

Ceratopsian Characteristics

Plant-eating *Yinlong* did not have the dramatic horns of later ceratopsians, or much of a frill. It is counted as part of the family because of its parrot-like beak, formed by a bony lump on its upper jaw. Later ceratopsians were much larger and moved on all fours, but *Yinlong* was small, bipedal, and speedy.

Yinlong had three-fingered hands at the end of short, slim arms. It had chunky, muscular back legs.

Yinlong had a deep, wide skull. The tip of the snout was like a parrot's beak.

Made in China

Chinese palaeontologist Xu Xing has named more dinosaurs than any living paleontologist. *Yinlong* and *Guanlong* owe their names to him, as well as the therizinosaur *Beipiaosaurus*, dromaeosaur *Sinornithosaurus* and birdlike *Mei*.

Beipiaosaurus was found near Beipiao, a city in northeastern China.

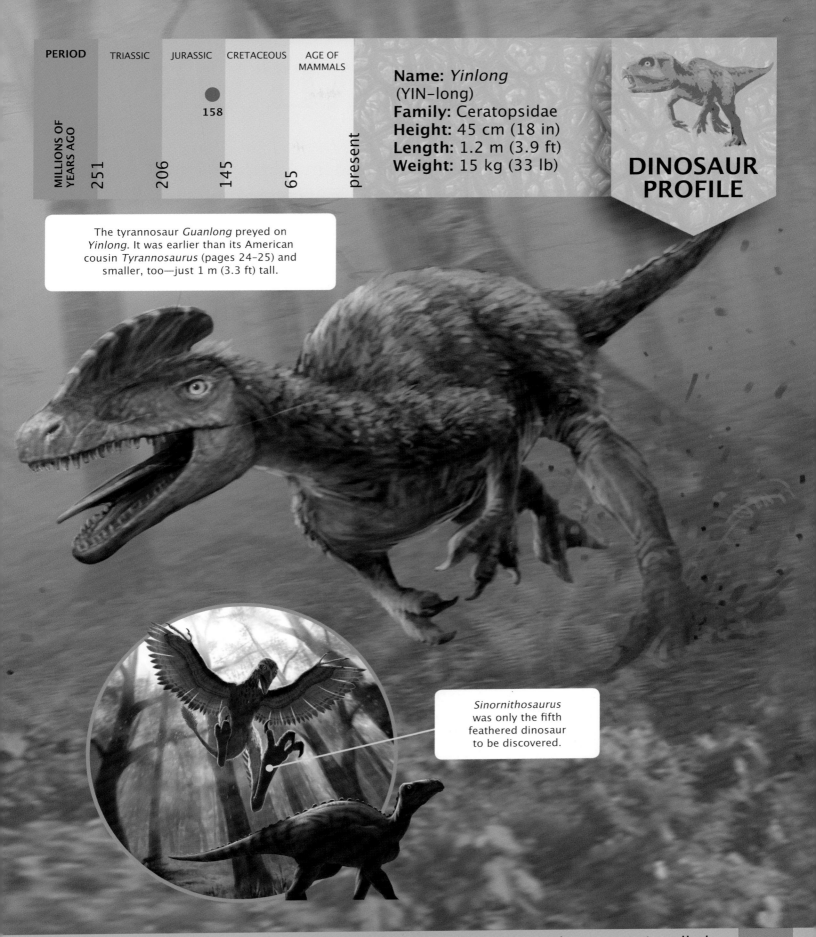

PERIOD	TRIASSIC	JURASSIC	CRETACEOUS	AGE OF MAMMALS	present
MILLIONS OF YEARS AGO	251	206	145	65	

158

Name: *Yinlong*
(YIN–long)
Family: Ceratopsidae
Height: 45 cm (18 in)
Length: 1.2 m (3.9 ft)
Weight: 15 kg (33 lb)

DINOSAUR PROFILE

The tyrannosaur *Guanlong* preyed on *Yinlong*. It was earlier than its American cousin *Tyrannosaurus* (pages 24–25) and smaller, too—just 1 m (3.3 ft) tall.

Sinornithosaurus was only the fifth feathered dinosaur to be discovered.

DID YOU KNOW? *Yinlong* was discovered in the Chinese province where a movie called *Crouching Tiger, Hidden Dragon* (2000) was filmed. Its name means "**hidden dragon**."

Psittacosaurus

Another early ceratopsian, *Psittacosaurus* lived in eastern Asia in the Early Cretaceous. Its name means "parrot lizard." Paleontologists have uncovered and studied hundreds of *Psittacosaurus* fossils and identified at least 14 different species.

Differences and Similarities

Psittacosaurus varied in size—the smallest species was a third smaller than the largest—but they were all roughly the same shape. They had a distinctive, rounded skull that could have housed a large brain. They also had large eye sockets. Paleontologists think that *Psittacosaurus* had good senses of sight and smell.

Psittacosaurus had defensive horns sticking on from its cheeks.

It is possible that only some species had tail bristles, or even just some individuals.

Bristled Tail

In 2002 paleontologists announced the discovery of the most perfectly preserved *Psittacosaurus* fossil yet. It had very detailed skin impressions and, excitingly, 16-cm (6.3-in) bristles on its tail. Since then, more individuals with bristles have been found.

This fossil shows the bristles sticking out from the tail.

DID YOU KNOW? Early Cretaceous rocks in East Asia contain so many *Psittacosaurus* fossils that they are called the *Psittacosaurus* **biochron**.

PERIOD	TRIASSIC	JURASSIC	CRETACEOUS	AGE OF MAMMALS	
MILLIONS OF YEARS AGO	251	206	145	65	present

112

Name: *Psittacosaurus*
(SIT–uh–ko–SAWR–us)
Family: Psittacosauridae
Height: 60 cm (23.6 in)
Length: 2 m (6.6 ft)
Weight: 20 kg (44 lb)

DINOSAUR PROFILE

Psittacosaurus's rounded and flattened beak was strong enough to crack tough seeds and nuts.

Birdlike *Sinovenator* hunted in packs. It was a troodontid (pages 20–21).

Zuniceratops

Sometimes called the missing link between the early ceratopsians and the later ones, *Zuniceratops* had a large frill, two brow horns, but no nose horn. It lived in what is now New Mexico about ten million years before its nose-horned cousins appeared.

Face Features

Zuniceratops had a long snout with a bony ridge along it. It fed on cones, shrubs, and bark, which it stripped from tree trunks with its beaky mouth. Its cheek bones stuck out to the sides, and might have been tipped with tiny horns.

Zuniceratops is the earliest known ceratopsian with brow horns.

The Fringed Heads

Zuniceratops and the ceratopsians belonged to a group of dinosaurs called the marginocephalians, or "fringed heads," that had a thick, bony fringe at the back of the skull. The pachycephalosaurs were marginocephalians, too. Named after *Pachycephalosaurus* (pages 80–81), they include *Stegoceras* (pages 72–73) and *Stygimoloch* (pages 84–85).

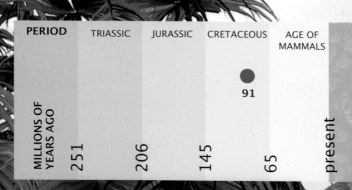

PERIOD	TRIASSIC	JURASSIC	CRETACEOUS	AGE OF MAMMALS

MILLIONS OF YEARS AGO: 251 · 206 · 145 · 65 · present

91

Name: *Zuniceratops*
(ZOO-nee-SEH-ruh-tops)
Family: Ceratopsidae
Height: 3 m (10 ft)
Length: 3.5 m (11.5 ft)
Weight: 150 kg (350 lb)

DINOSAUR PROFILE

Zuniceratops is named after the Zuni people, a tribe of Native Americans that live in New Mexico, U.S.A.

Zuniceratops is known from just one skull and a handful of other bones.

The brow horns carried on growing throughout its life.

Zuniceratops walked on all fours. It probably lived in herds to protect itself against theropods.

Holes in the frill bone kept it as light as possible. A solid frill would have made the skull too heavy for the neck to support.

DID YOU KNOW? The first *Zuniceratops* fossil was found by an **eight-year-old boy**!

Stegoceras

A small, bipedal plant eater, *Stegoceras* lived in North America around 75 mya. As in all pachycephalosaurs (thick-headed dinosaurs), *Stegoceras*'s skull had extra-thick bone at the top. Its name means "horn roof."

Dome Details

Stegoceras's skull dome would have protected the brain if the dinosaur charged headfirst. Most experts no longer believe that pachycephalosaurs fought each other head-to-head, but they could have still headbutted attackers and rivals. Perhaps the dome also helped to identify *Stegoceras* males and females or may have been used for display.

With big eyes and complex nasal cavaties, *Stegoceras* would have had good senses of sight and smell.

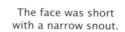

The face was short with a narrow snout.

PERIOD	TRIASSIC	JURASSIC	CRETACEOUS	AGE OF MAMMALS
MILLIONS OF YEARS AGO	251	206	145	65	present

75

Name: *Stegoceras*
(Steg–OSS–er–us)
Family: Pachycephalosauridae
Height: 65 cm (25.6 in)
Length: 2.25 m (7.4 ft)
Weight: 30 kg (66 lb)

DINOSAUR PROFILE

The skull probably started out flat and became more domed as *Stegoceras* grew.

First Fossils

Stegoceras fossils were first discovered in the Dinosaur Park Formation (page 58) by the Canadian paleontologist Lawrence Lambe. It is one of the earliest-known pachycephalosaurs. Teeth found near the first find were also thought to belong to *Stegoceras*, but were later identified as belonging to a very different dinosaur—*Troodon* (pages 20–21).

Stegoceras's back legs were about three times longer than its arms.

Early reconstructions show *Stegoceras* with a straight neck. In reality, it was curved.

DID YOU KNOW? Two **species** of *Stegoceras* have been discovered—one lived in the far north, in Alberta, Canada, and one was found in New Mexico, southwestern U.S.A.

Styracosaurus

Unlike its cousin *Triceratops* (pages 82–83), *Styracosaurus* did not battle by locking horns. It did not even have brow horns. However, it did have an impressive nose horn and a showy selection of spikes around its neck frill.

Weighty Attacker

Styracosaurus's name means "spiked lizard." The size and condition of its spikes were important for impressing would-be mates and scaring off rivals. Faced with an enemy, *Styracosaurus* probably charged at it side-on, relying on its powerful shoulders and all the force of its 3-tonne (3.3-ton) body.

Styracosaurus may have pumped blood into its fleshy frill to "blush." This could have been a signal to others of its species that it was ready to mate.

Shared Environment

Herbivorous *Styracosaurus* was another dinosaur discovered in Canada's Dinosaur Park Formation (page 58). Other ceratopsians also lived in its habitat of swamps and floodplains, including *Centrosaurus* and *Chasmosaurus*. Predators included the tyrannosaurs *Albertosaurus* and *Gorgosaurus*.

Fearsome tyrannosaur *Albertosaurus* preyed on young *Styracosaurus*.

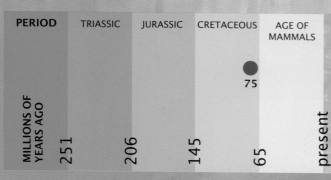

PERIOD	TRIASSIC	JURASSIC	CRETACEOUS	AGE OF MAMMALS	present
MILLIONS OF YEARS AGO	251	206	145	65	

75

Name: *Styracosaurus*
(Stih–RAK–uh–SAWR–us)
Family: Ceratopsidae
Height: 1.8 m (6 ft)
Length: 5.5 m (18 ft)
Weight: 3 tonnes (3.3 tons)

DINOSAUR PROFILE

DID YOU KNOW? No one is sure how tall *Styracosaurus*'s **nose horn** was. It may have been up to 60 cm (2 ft) long.

Styracosaurus had a tall, straight nose horn but no brow horns.

The neck frill had at least four pairs of long spikes. There could be smaller spikes at the base of the frill, too.

Hollow "windows" in the bone kept the neck frill light.

Styracosaurus's short, stubby legs supported a bulky body, like a rhino's.

Achelousaurus

Achelousaurus was a medium-sized ceratopsian that lived in North America in the Late Cretaceous. It had two short cheek spikes and a pair of longer spikes at the top of its neck frill.

Wavy-Edged Frill

Achelousaurus belonged to the group of ceratopsians known as the centrosaurines, which were named after *Centrosaurus*. Their name, meaning "pointed lizards," refers to their distinguishing feature—the small hornlets dotted around the edge of their neck frill.

Achelousaurus had raised bony areas, called bosses, along its snout and above its eyes.

PERIOD	TRIASSIC	JURASSIC	CRETACEOUS	AGE OF MAMMALS
MILLIONS OF YEARS AGO	251	206	145	65 present

74.5

Name: *Achelousaurus* (Ah-KEL-oo-SAWR-us)
Family: Ceratopsidae
Height: 2.7 m (8.9 ft)
Length: 6 m (20 ft)
Weight: 3 tonnes (3.3 tons)

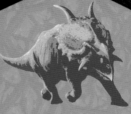

DINOSAUR PROFILE

Achelousaurus's skull was more than 1.6 m (5.2 ft) long from the tip of its spikes to the end of its beaky snout.

Horns and Lumps

Achelousaurus was closely related to another ceratopsian, *Einiosaurus*. Both had spiky frill margins and two longer spikes at the top of the frill; both had bony lumps, or bosses, instead of brow horns. *Einiosaurus* still had a nose horn—it curved downward very distinctively. *Achelousaurus* had a bony lump on its nose instead of a horn.

This *Achelousaurus* skull was dug up in Montana, U.S.A., in 1985 by the American paleontologist Jack Horner.

Achelousaurus used its ridged, parrot-like beak to break off tough plant stems.

DID YOU KNOW? *Achelousaurus* was named after the Greek river god Achelous, whose bull-like horns were pulled off by the hero **Heracles**.

Protoceratops

A spectacular fossil discovered in 1971 in the Gobi Desert, Mongolia, captured two dinosaurs locked in combat. They had been buried alive. One was the plant-eating, primitive ceratopsian *Protoceratops*; the other was the dromaeosaur *Velociraptor*.

Life in the Gobi

Many *Protoceratops* specimens have been found in the red sandstone of the Gobi Desert, including fossilized nests, eggs, and babies. During the Late Cretaceous, the Gobi was not as dry as it is now. There were probably seasonal floods.

Protoceratops and *Velociraptor* had been preserved in sand mid-fight. Experts believe they were caught up in a sudden sandstorm.

Protoceratops used its wide, spade-like claws to dig nests and burrows. It laid up to 15 eggs at a time.

Like all dromaeosaurs, *Velociraptor* had a killer curved claw on the second toe of each foot. It slashed at prey to make it bleed to death.

PERIOD	TRIASSIC	JURASSIC	CRETACEOUS	AGE OF MAMMALS	present
MILLIONS OF YEARS AGO	251	206	145	65	

73

Name: *Protoceratops* (Pro-toe-SEH-ruh-tops)
Family: Ceratopsidae
Height: 70 cm (27.6 in)
Length: 1.9 m (6.2 ft)
Weight: 180 kg (397 lb)

DINOSAUR PROFILE

This fossil of a newly hatched *Protoceratops andrewsi* was discovered in 1997.

Desert Discoveries

The first *Protoceratops* specimens were discovered in the 1920s by American paleontologist Roy Chapman Andrews, so they were given the species name *andrewsi*. In 2001, a second species was identified, *Protoceratops hellenikorhinus*. Unlike *Protoceratops andrewsi*, it had two nose horns, but no front teeth.

Protoceratops had a relatively large neck frill, probably for display.

Velociraptor was about the same size as *Protoceratops*.

Protoceratops's tough, horny beak was not powerful enough to damage *Velociraptor*.

DID YOU KNOW? The theropod *Oviraptor* got its name, meaning "**egg thief**," because experts once thought—mistakenly—that it stole *Protoceratops* eggs.

Pachycephalosaurus

The pachycephalosaurs are named after *Pachycephalosaurus*, a dome-headed dinosaur from Late Cretaceous North America. Paleontologists once thought that these plant-eaters bashed their heads together like goats. However, it is unlikely that they fought each other head-to-head.

Pachycephalosaurus walked and ran on two legs, but would have foraged on all fours.

Protective Helmet

The solid bone at the top of the skull protected *Pachycephalosaurus*'s delicate brain when it charged headfirst at full speed. The bone was 25 cm (10 in) thick in places.

Pachycephalosaurus's jaw had tiny, sharp teeth for eating soft fruit, seeds, and young leaves.

PERIOD	TRIASSIC	JURASSIC	CRETACEOUS	AGE OF MAMMALS	
MILLIONS OF YEARS AGO	251	206	145	68 / 65	present

Name: *Pachycephalosaurus*
(Pak-ee-SEF-uh-lo-SAWR-us)
Family: Pachycephalosauridae
Height: 1.8 m (5.9 ft)
Length: 4.5 m (15 ft)
Weight: 450 kg (992 lb)

DINOSAUR PROFILE

DID YOU KNOW? *Pachycephalosaurus* is the **largest-known** pachycephalosaur.

Large eyes gave *Pachycephalosaurus* good binocular vision.

Pachycephalosaurus used its head to charge into rivals' thighs.

There was a circle of bony spikes around the bottom of the skull dome; there were also spikes at the end of the snout.

Pachycephalosaurus had long legs and short arms. It was not a fast runner.

Fossil Discoveries

Pachycephalosaurus was named in 1931. Not many fossils have been found—just one skull, some skull roofs, and a few other bones. In 2016 paleontologists announced that they had found skulls from two baby *Pachycephalosaurus* at the Hell Creek Formation in Montana, U.S.A.

Triceratops

The neck frill might have helped *Triceratops* keep its temperature steady. It was also for display.

One of the biggest ceratopsians, *Triceratops* lived right at the end of the Cretaceous in what is now North America. Its most striking feature was its three horns—a longer pair above its eyes and a shorter one on its nose.

Skull Features

Triceratops's skull was massive. Its horns and neck frill were both used for display—showing off to possible mates, fighting rivals, and perhaps even allowing herd members to identify each other. The dinosaur also used its horns to defend against predatory tyrannosaurs.

Triceratops's skull was around 2 m (6.6 ft) long—about a quarter of its total body length.

PERIOD	TRIASSIC	JURASSIC	CRETACEOUS	AGE OF MAMMALS
MILLIONS OF YEARS AGO	251	206	145	65 ... present

67

Name: *Triceratops* (Try–SEH–ruh–tops)
Family: Ceratopsidae
Height: 3 m (10 ft)
Length: 8.5 m (28 ft)
Weight: 8 tonnes (8.8 tons)

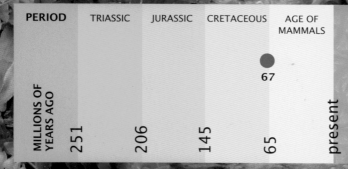

DINOSAUR PROFILE

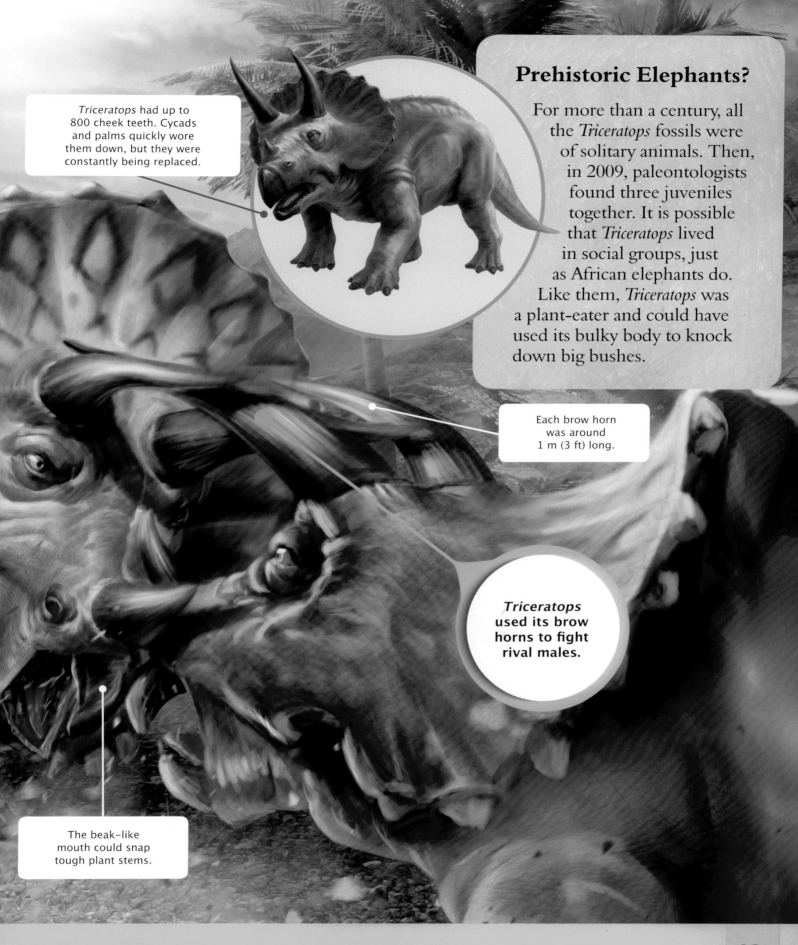

Prehistoric Elephants?

For more than a century, all the *Triceratops* fossils were of solitary animals. Then, in 2009, paleontologists found three juveniles together. It is possible that *Triceratops* lived in social groups, just as African elephants do. Like them, *Triceratops* was a plant-eater and could have used its bulky body to knock down big bushes.

Triceratops had up to 800 cheek teeth. Cycads and palms quickly wore them down, but they were constantly being replaced.

Each brow horn was around 1 m (3 ft) long.

Triceratops used its brow horns to fight rival males.

The beak–like mouth could snap tough plant stems.

DID YOU KNOW? Some fossils of *Triceratops* skulls have *Tyrannosaurus* **bite marks!**

Stygimoloch

Discovered in the Hell Creek Formation of Montana, U.S.A., *Stygimoloch* was first described in 1983. Since then, paleontologists have argued about whether this plant-eating pachycephalosaur is a species in its own right or just a juvenile version of *Pachycephalosaurus* (pages 80–81).

Bizarre Beast

Like *Pachycephalosaurus*, *Stygimoloch* had a dome-shaped skull surrounded by bony horns. It had more horny bumps on the top of its snout. Its otherworldly appearance is reflected in its name, which combines "Styx," the river of the dead in Greek mythology, and "Moloch," a Canaanite god worshipped in the Middle East around 1500–1000 BCE.

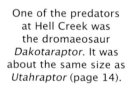

One of the predators at Hell Creek was the dromaeosaur *Dakotaraptor*. It was about the same size as *Utahraptor* (page 14).

Stygimoloch's skull was about 46 cm (18 in) long.

Part of *Stygimoloch*'s skull, showing some of its horns.

Horns and Growth

American dinosaur expert Jack Horner was one of the first to suggest that *Stygimoloch* was a young *Pachycephalosaurus*. He also thought that *Dracorex* was an earlier growth stage of the same dinosaur. *Pachycephalosaurus* had fewer horns than *Dracorex* or *Stygimoloch*. If Horner's argument is true, it must mean that the dinosaur lost horns as it aged, but that its dome grew larger.

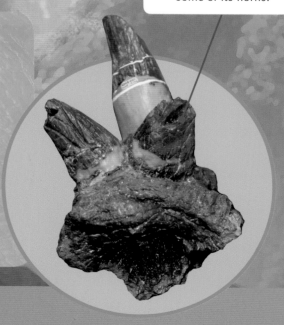

PERIOD	TRIASSIC	JURASSIC	CRETACEOUS	AGE OF MAMMALS
MILLIONS OF YEARS AGO	251	206	145	65 present

66

Name: *Stygimoloch*
(Stij-ih-MOL-ock)
Family: Pachycephalosauridae
Height: 1.2 m (4 ft)
Length: 3 m (10 ft)
Weight: 78 kg (172 lb)

DINOSAUR PROFILE

Stygimoloch had a cluster of spikes at the back of the head. There was one pair of longer spikes, up to 15 cm (5.9 in) long, and a few smaller ones.

Stygimoloch had spikes on its cheeks, too, perhaps for protection.

DID YOU KNOW? There is one species of *Dracorex*—*Dracorex hogwartsia* ("dragon king of Hogwarts"). It is named after the school of magic in the **Harry Potter** books.

85

Scutellosaurus

Appearing in the Early Jurassic, *Scutellosaurus* was an ancestor of the later shielded dinosaurs, such as *Ankylosaurus* (pages 104–105) and *Stegosaurus* (pages 92–93). The name *Scutellosaurus* means "lizard with little shields."

Little Darter

Scutellosaurus was a plant-eater that lived in what is now Arizona, in the southern United States. Small and lightly built, it had longer back legs than front ones, so it probably moved around on two legs. Its small skull housed a small brain.

The speedy theropod *Coelophysis* would have hunted *Scutellosaurus*.

The Shield Bearers

Scutellosaurus belonged to a group of dinosaurs called the thyreophorans, or "shield bearers." Their skin had evolved to protect them from attack. Early thyreophorans, such as *Scutellosaurus* and *Scelidosaurus* (pages 88–89), simply had bony bumps, called osteoderms. By the Late Cretaceous, the group included ankylosaurs and stegosaurs, which had elaborate plates and spikes.

Scutellosaurus probably went down on all fours to eat shrubby plants.

Scutellosaurus's back was studded with bony scales called osteoderms.

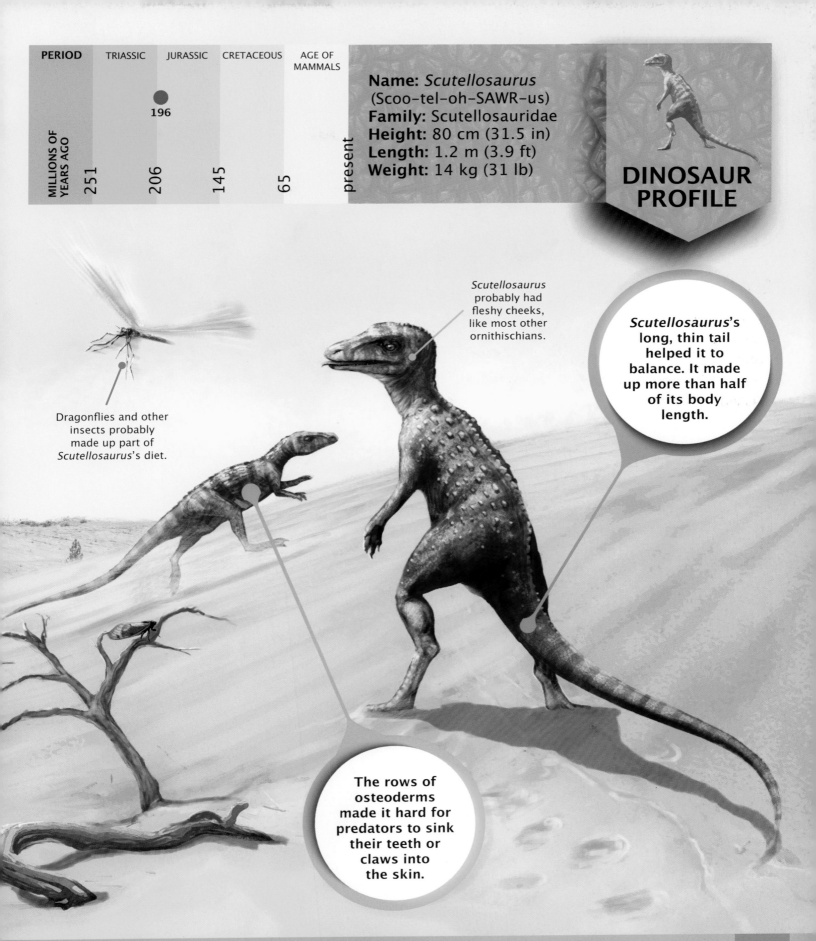

PERIOD	TRIASSIC	JURASSIC	CRETACEOUS	AGE OF MAMMALS	present
MILLIONS OF YEARS AGO	251	206	145	65	

196

Name: *Scutellosaurus*
(Scoo-tel-oh-SAWR-us)
Family: Scutellosauridae
Height: 80 cm (31.5 in)
Length: 1.2 m (3.9 ft)
Weight: 14 kg (31 lb)

DINOSAUR PROFILE

Scutellosaurus probably had fleshy cheeks, like most other ornithischians.

Dragonflies and other insects probably made up part of *Scutellosaurus*'s diet.

Scutellosaurus's long, thin tail helped it to balance. It made up more than half of its body length.

The rows of osteoderms made it hard for predators to sink their teeth or claws into the skin.

DID YOU KNOW? *Scutellosaurus* is the only known shielded dinosaur that moved around on **two legs**. The rest were quadrupedal.

Scelidosaurus

Another of the early thyreophorans, *Scelidosaurus* was discovered in Dorset, southern England. Unlike *Scutellosaurus* (pages 86–87), it walked on all fours. Its bony plates (or scutes) were larger, too—more like those of later dinosaurs in the group.

Teeth and Jaws

Scelidosaurus had a small head, just 20 cm (7.9 in) long, and a beaky mouth. When it was first found, paleontologists thought it was a fish-eater, because of its long teeth. In reality, it ate plants. Its jaw only moved up and down, not side to side, so it had to bite through leaves rather than grinding them.

Legs and Toes

Scelidosaurus was named by Richard Owen, the same scientist who came up with the word "dinosaur." *Scelidosaurus* means "limb lizard" and refers to the dinosaur's stout back legs. The feet had four long toes with blunt claws.

Flying reptiles called pterosaurs (pages 118–125) lived in the Mesozoic.

The beaky mouth was used to eat ferns and conifers.

Osteoderms protected the back and tail, but not the legs or underside.

Scelidosaurus had a large stomach for breaking down plant matter.

Scelidosaurus walked on all fours. Its back legs were longer than its front ones, so its head was close to the ground.

This image shows one of the first *Scelidosaurus* finds—an incomplete skull. The snout tip is missing.

PERIOD	TRIASSIC	JURASSIC	CRETACEOUS	AGE OF MAMMALS
MILLIONS OF YEARS AGO	251	206 ● 190	145	65	present

Name: *Scelidosaurus*
(Skel–ee–doe–SAWR–us)
Family: Scelidosauridae
Height: 1.5 m (5 ft)
Length: 4 m (13 ft)
Weight: 270 kg (595 lb)

DINOSAUR PROFILE

DID YOU KNOW? In 1858 a *Scelidosaurus* skeleton was found—it was the earliest **complete** dinosaur fossil.

Tuojiangosaurus

Sometimes called the Asian *Stegosaurus* (pages 92–93), *Tuojiangosaurus* lived in China in the Late Jurassic. It was a typical stegosaur, with plates along the length of its back and deadly tail spikes.

Sichuan Stegosaurs

Tuojiangosaurus means "Tuo River lizard" after the river in Sichuan Province, southwestern China, where the dinosaur was discovered. Other stegosaurs shared its habitat. Two of these—*Chungkingosaurus* and *Chialingosaurus*, both just 4 m (13 ft) long—may have been *Tuojiangosaurus* juveniles, not separate species.

Tuojiangosaurus held its tail off the ground. It could swing its sharp tail spikes at predators.

Tuojiangosaurus had a double row of horn-covered plates, just like *Kentrosaurus* (pages 94–95).

PERIOD	TRIASSIC	JURASSIC	CRETACEOUS	AGE OF MAMMALS	present
MILLIONS OF YEARS AGO	251	206	145	65	

160

Name: *Tuojiangosaurus* (Too-YANG-oh-SAWR-us)
Family: Stegosauridae
Height: 2 m (6.6 ft)
Length: 7 m (23 ft)
Weight: 1.5 tonnes (1.7 tons)

DINOSAUR PROFILE

The plates were different sizes and shapes. The largest were over the hip; they grew smaller toward the head.

Eating Habits

Tuojiangosaurus browsed on low plants. While it was eating, its head stayed slightly dipped, helped by the shorter front legs. The jaws contained at least 25 small teeth for snipping off vegetation.

The snout was long and shallow with a beaky tip.

Tuojiangosaurus ate low–growing ferns and cycads.

Early reconstructions of stegosaurs sometimes positioned the front legs sprawling out to the sides. In fact, they were held directly under the body.

DID YOU KNOW? *Tuojiangosaurus* was named in 1977. Its fossilized remains had been discovered by **construction workers** building a dam.

Stegosaurus

Stegosaurs are all named after *Stegosaurus*, which ranged across North America and Europe during the Middle Jurassic. This herbivore had a small head, diamond-shaped plates along its back, and a defensive, spiky tail.

Lethal Weapon

The group of spikes at the end of a stegosaur's tail is called a thagomizer. It was *Stegosaurus*'s only protection against predators. The dinosaur swung and flicked its tail, hoping to hit an attacker and inflict serious damage.

Stegosaurus's skull was long and narrow.

Unlike other known stegosaurs, *Stegosaurus*'s plates were staggered instead of in pairs.

All about Plates

Early reconstructions of *Stegosaurus* had its plates flat on top of its body—that is how the dinosaur got its name, which means "roofed lizard." Paleontologists now know that the plates stood upright, making the dinosaur look bigger than it was. They were almost certainly for display, but they may have also helped *Stegosaurus* to regulate its body temperature.

Stegosaurus probably used its plates to show off to other members of the same species.

PERIOD	TRIASSIC	JURASSIC	CRETACEOUS	AGE OF MAMMALS

MILLIONS OF YEARS AGO

251   206   145   65   present

153

Name: *Stegosaurus*
(STEG-uh-SAWR-us)
Family: Stegosauridae
Height: 2.75 m (9 ft)
Length: 9 m (30 ft)
Weight: 5 tonnes (5.5 tons)

DINOSAUR PROFILE

Stegosaurus's small skull housed a hotdog-shaped brain.

Ornitholestes hunted in packs.

Stegosaurus could not move fast because of its short front legs. Its top speed was 7 km/h (4.3 mph).

Ornitholestes was a 12.6-kg (27.8-lb) theropod that lived in North America at the same time as *Stegosaurus*.

DID YOU KNOW? *Stegosaurus*'s **plates** were up to 60 cm (23.6 in) tall.

Kentrosaurus

The small stegosaur *Kentrosaurus* lived in what is now Tanzania about 152 mya. It shared its wet, swampy forest habitat with one of the giants of the plant-eating dinosaurs, *Giraffatitan* (page 33).

Plenty of Plants

There was no shortage of food in Late Jurassic East Africa, so *Kentrosaurus* did not need to compete with *Giraffatitan*. Plants flourished in the wet, tropical climate. *Kentrosaurus* fed low to the ground, using its beaky mouth to snap up vegetation.

As in *Stegosaurus* (pages 92–93), the plates along the back may have helped *Kentrosaurus* lose or soak up heat.

Kentrosaurus had a narrow, pointed snout.

Kentrosaurus's tropical environment had two seasons: dry and wet.

DID YOU KNOW? *Kentrosaurus* means "**spiked reptile**."

Name: *Kentrosaurus*
(KEN–truh–SAWR–us)
Family: Stegosauridae
Height: 1.8 m (6 ft)
Length: 4.5 m (15 ft)
Weight: 1 tonne (1.1 tons)

DINOSAUR PROFILE

Kentrosaurus could swing its tail back 180 degrees to target an attacker alongside its own body.

From Tendaguru

Kentrosaurus was discovered in the Tendaguru Formation. No complete skeleton has been found, but paleontologists have been able to piece different specimens together. They have found nearly a thousand *Kentrosaurus* fossils in the Tendaguru rock.

More than half of *Kentrosaurus*'s body length was made up of its tail.

Minmi

The small ankylosaur *Minmi* lived in what is now Queensland, Australia, around 115 mya. It is named after Minmi Crossing, a landmark near the place where it was first discovered in 1964.

Speed and Shields

Unlike most slow-moving ankylosaurs, *Minmi* was probably a fast runner. It had extra bones across its spine that could have anchored extra muscles. If that really is what those "paravertebrae" (across bones) were for, *Minmi* could have outrun many predators. When it encountered a speedy hunter, it relied on its protective plates to discourage them from attacking.

All-Over Protection

Most ankylosaurs had short, stubby legs. This meant that their softer-skinned bellies were held low to the ground, where they were hard to reach. *Minmi* was different. It had relatively long legs, but it also had bony plates all over its body, even on its underside.

Minmi had long legs for an ankylosaur.

PERIOD	TRIASSIC	JURASSIC	CRETACEOUS	AGE OF MAMMALS
MILLIONS OF YEARS AGO	251	206	145 ● 115	65 present

Name: *Minmi*
(MIN–mee)
Family: Ankylosauridae
Height: 1 m (3.3 ft)
Length: 3 m (9.8 ft)
Weight: 300 kg (661 lb)

DINOSAUR PROFILE

Early Cretaceous Queensland was an island, cut off from the rest of Australia.

Minmi lived in forests and floodplains. It ate ferns, and leaves, fruit and seeds from the first flowering plants.

Protective plates covered its back and belly.

The skull was shaped like an arrowhead.

Minmi had strong back legs for sprinting through the undergrowth.

DID YOU KNOW? *Minmi* had the **shortest name** of any dinosaur for more than two decades. Today, *Mei* has the shortest name.

Sauropelta

The 90-cm-
(35-in-) long
shoulder spikes
helped make
Sauropelta look
bigger than it
really was.

Living across North America in the Early Cretaceous,
plant-eating *Sauropelta* was a kind of ankylosaur.
Large, bony studs, called osteoderms, shielded its
back. Two long, defensive spikes stuck out from its
shoulders and it had shorter spikes along its sides.

Well-Defended

Sauropelta means 'shielded lizard." Its
bones and spikes were essential protection
against the predators of the day, such as
Acrocanthosaurus, a relative of *Allosaurus*
(pages 8–9), and *Deinonychus* (pages 14–15).
Even with their fearsome jaws, *Sauropelta*'s
studded skin was too hard to bite through.

This section of fossilized
Sauropelta skin shows
the protective, bony
osteoderms, or scutes.

Nodosaurs

Sauropelta is the earliest known
nodosaur. Named after *Nodosaurus*,
the tank-like nodosaurs were
ankylosaurs that did not have tail
clubs but that had certain other
features, including a bony bump
over each eye, another bump at
the base of the skull, and spikes
on the lower jaw.
Edmontonia (pages
100–101) was a
nodosaur, too.

The flattened skull
was made up of
plates that had
fused together.

PERIOD	TRIASSIC	JURASSIC	CRETACEOUS	AGE OF MAMMALS	present
MILLIONS OF YEARS AGO	251	206	145	65	

108

Name: *Sauropelta*
(SAWR–oh–PEL–tah)
Family: Nodosauridae
Height: 2.4 m (8 ft)
Length: 5.2 m (17.1 ft)
Weight: 1.5 tonnes (1.65 tons)

DINOSAUR PROFILE

The long tail contained more than 40 vertebrae (spine bones) and made up half of the dinosaur's total body length.

Sauropelta's back was covered with bony bumps called osteoderms.

DID YOU KNOW? Hundreds of fossilized **dinosaur footprints** discovered in Alberta, Canada, were almost certainly made by herds of *Sauropelta*.

Edmontonia

One of the largest nodosaurs, herbivorous *Edmontonia* lived across North America in the Late Cretaceous. Pyramid-shaped spikes covered its back, while forward-facing shoulder spikes protected the head and neck. Sometimes, these spikes split to create even deadlier forked tips.

Shoulder Power

Edmontonia's shoulder spikes carried on growing throughout its life. They gave some protection if the dinosaur had to charge past an attacking theropod. However, their main purpose was for fighting rivals. *Edmontonia* males probably battled over territory and mates. The ones with larger shoulder spikes would have had more status.

Edmontonia has been found in Canada's Dinosaur Park Formation, along with the ankylosaur *Scolosaurus* (left) and nodosaur *Panoplosaurus* (right).

PERIOD	TRIASSIC	JURASSIC	CRETACEOUS	AGE OF MAMMALS
MILLIONS OF YEARS AGO	251	206	145	65	present

72

Name: *Edmontonia*
(Ed–mon–TOE–nee–uh)
Family: Nodosauridae
Height: 1.8 m (5.9 ft)
Length: 6.6 m (22 ft)
Weight: 3 tonnes (3.3 tons)

DINOSAUR PROFILE

DID YOU KNOW? *Edmontonia* is named after **Edmonton**, the capital city of the Canadian province of Alberta, in western Canada.

Stories in Rock

As *Edmontonia* was widespread, its fossils have been found in different rock formations across North America. The first identified *Edmontonia* was discovered in 1928 in Alberta's Edmonton Formation (since renamed the Horseshoe Canyon Formation).

Each shoulder spike was made from strong, dense bone.

Rival *Edmontonia* would barge at each other, shoulder to shoulder.

Edmontonia's skull was about 50 cm (19.7 in) long. It was protected by osteoderms that had fused together to form a bony helmet.

Euoplocephalus

One of the largest ankylosaurs, plant-eating *Euoplocephalus* had a spike-covered body and a wide, heavy tail club. Its short legs carried its body low to the ground, leaving its vulnerable belly almost impossible for any attacker to reach.

Solo Life

Euoplocephalus lived in what is now Canada during the Late Cretaceous. Most fossils have been found on their own, so paleontologists believe that *Euoplocephalus* was not a herd animal. They think it lived alone, like today's hippopotamus.

Horns poked out from the back of the head.

Most ankylosaurs had four toes on their back feet, but *Euoplocephalus* had just three.

PERIOD	TRIASSIC	JURASSIC	CRETACEOUS	AGE OF MAMMALS
MILLIONS OF YEARS AGO	251	206	145	65	present

76

Name: *Euoplocephalus* (You-op-luh-SEF-uh-lus)
Family: Ankylosauridae
Height: 1.8 m (6 ft)
Length: 6 m (20 ft)
Weight: 2 tonnes (2.2 tons)

DINOSAUR PROFILE

Safe Skull

Euoplocephalus had bony "lids" over its eyes that could close to shade out the sun. Spiky horns protected the back and sides of the head. Most importantly, the top of the skull was double-thickness, because it had fused with the plates that covered it.

Bony plates protected the top of the skull.

Excluding the beaky mouth, the skull was 35 cm (13.8 in) long.

The vertebrae at the end of the tail were fused to create a stiff "handle" for the heavy tail club.

The body was very wide—about 2.4 m (7.9 ft) across.

This young *Euoplocephalus* is hitching a ride across the swamp on its mother's back.

DID YOU KNOW? *Euoplocephalus* had complicated passages in its nose, so it probably had a good sense of smell.

Ankylosaurus

Ankylosaurs all take their name from *Ankylosaurus* ("fused lizard"). It was the largest ankylosaur and one of the best-protected, with a large tail club of solid bone.

Terrifying Threats

Ankylosaurus lived in North America at the end of the Cretaceous. This herbivore shared its habitat with one of the most terrifying hunters of all time—*Tyrannosaurus* (pages 24–25). However, an adult *Ankylosaurus* could have swung its tail club with enough force to break *Tyrannosaurus*'s leg.

Big Head

Ankylosaurus's skull had many air passages running through it that made it bulge out at the sides. Paleontologists are still not sure what these passages were for. They may have helped with the dinosaur's sense of smell or they may have amplified its calls (made them louder).

Four head spikes protected *Ankylosaurus*'s face.

DID YOU KNOW? *Ankylosaurus* had a very large, flexible **tongue**.

PERIOD	TRIASSIC	JURASSIC	CRETACEOUS	AGE OF MAMMALS	
MILLIONS OF YEARS AGO	251	206	145	67 ● 65	present

Name: *Ankylosaurus*
(Ang–KILE–uh–SAWR–us)
Family: Ankylosauridae
Height: 1.7 m (5.6 ft)
Length: 6.25 m (20.5 ft)
Weight: 6 tonnes (6.6 tons)

DINOSAUR PROFILE

Hundreds of bite–proof bony plates covered *Ankylosaurus*'s upper body.

The tail club was made of fused bone.

Ankylosaurus's jaw housed tiny teeth.

Plesiosaurus

Many types of reptile lived in Mesozoic oceans. The plesiosaurs were a group of long-necked swimming reptiles that first appeared in the Late Triassic and died out at the end of the Cretaceous. They are named after *Plesiosaurus* (the "close lizard").

Life in the Water

Plesiosaurus lived in shallow waters, close to the coast. It's possible it came ashore to lay its eggs, like today's turtles. It could not have moved quickly on land, because it had flippers instead of legs. Plesiosaurs evolved from nothosaurs, Triassic, four-legged reptiles whose feet had adapted to swimming in the water by being webbed and paddle-like.

Kaiwhekea was one of the last plesiosaurs. A specialist squid hunter, it grew to 7 m (23 ft) long.

Meyerasaurus lived in the Early Jurassic. It was about the same length as *Plesiosaurus*.

Short-Necked Cousins

Not all plesiosaurs had long necks. Pliosaurs, including *Pliosaurus* (page 110), *Kronosaurus* (pages 110–111) and *Meyerasaurus*, were plesiosaurs with shorter necks and bigger heads. Pliosaurs also had slightly larger back flippers than front ones (in most plesiosaurs, the front flippers were larger). All plesiosaurs shared the same feeding technique, however—snapping up fish and squid as they moved their head from side to side.

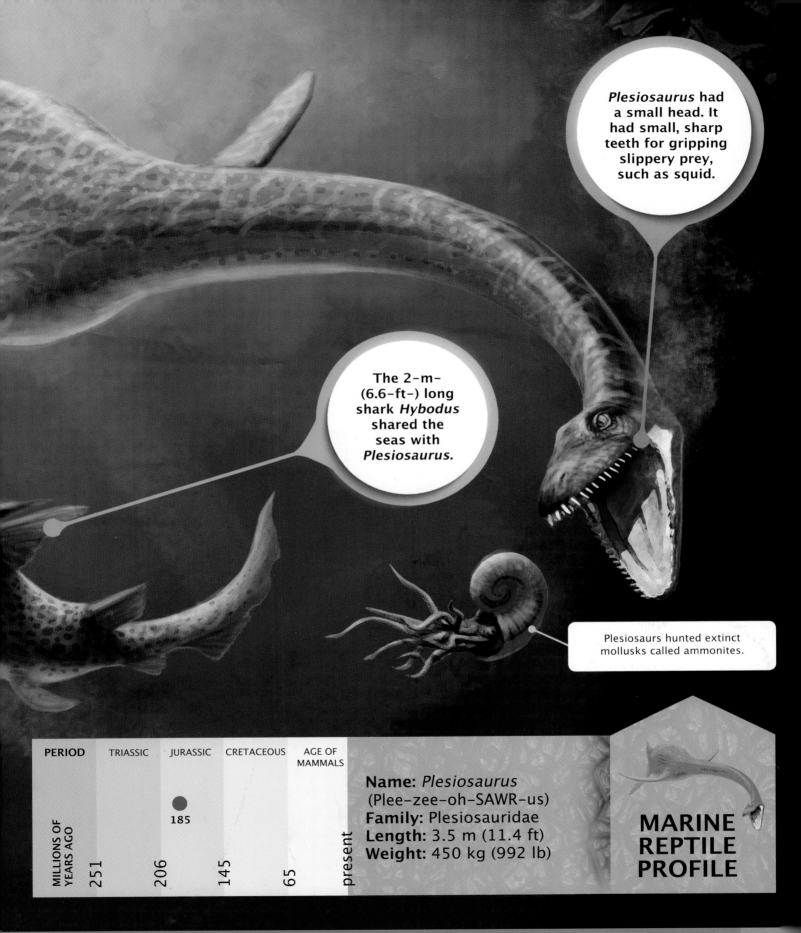

Plesiosaurus had a small head. It had small, sharp teeth for gripping slippery prey, such as squid.

The 2-m- (6.6-ft-) long shark *Hybodus* shared the seas with *Plesiosaurus.*

Plesiosaurs hunted extinct mollusks called ammonites.

PERIOD	TRIASSIC	JURASSIC	CRETACEOUS	AGE OF MAMMALS
MILLIONS OF YEARS AGO	251	206 ● 185	145	65 present

Name: *Plesiosaurus* (Plee-zee-oh-SAWR-us)
Family: Plesiosauridae
Length: 3.5 m (11.4 ft)
Weight: 450 kg (992 lb)

MARINE REPTILE PROFILE

DID YOU KNOW? The 19th-century fossil collector **Mary Anning** found the first *Plesiosaurus* in southern England in 1821. It was an almost-complete skeleton.

Temnodontosaurus

Streamlined like dolphins and usually fast-moving, ichthyosaurs were large marine reptiles that first appeared in the Late Triassic and survived until the Late Cretaceous. *Temnodontosaurus* was one of the biggest ichthyosaurs, at 12 m (39 ft). Most species were around 3 m (9.8 ft) long.

Air, Land, and Sea

Ichthyosaurs had to come up for air because they could not breathe underwater—but they did not need to come ashore to lay their eggs. Like some snakes today, ichthyosaurs were viviparous. In other words, their eggs developed inside their body and then the animals gave birth to live young.

The small, sharp teeth were perfectly suited to gripping slippery fish.

Shonisaurus was massive and slow-moving. Unlike most ichthyosaurs, it did not have a dorsal (back) fin.

PERIOD	TRIASSIC	JURASSIC	CRETACEOUS	AGE OF MAMMALS
MILLIONS OF YEARS AGO	251	206 ● 182	145	65 present

Name: *Temnodontosaurus* (Tem-noh-DON-tuh-SAWR-us)
Family: Temnodontosauridae
Length: 12 m (39 ft)
Weight: 4.5 tonnes (5 tons)

MARINE REPTILE PROFILE

Like most ichthyosaurs, *Temnodontosaurus* swam at high speeds. It moved its tail from side to side to propel itself through the water.

Hunting Accessories

Temnodontosaurus's name means "cutting tooth lizard." Its long, narrow jaw was packed with small, sharp teeth. However, this ichthyosaur is better-known for its huge eyes. In one species, *Temnodontosaurus platyodon*, these were 20 cm (8 in) across.

Temnodontosaurus's enormous eyes let in plenty of light, allowing the hunter to see in the ocean gloom.

Cast of *Temnodontosaurus platyodon*'s skull

DID YOU KNOW? The **largest-known** ichthyosaur was 21-m (69-ft) *Shastasaurus*.

109

Kronosaurus

One of the largest pliosaurs, 10-m- (33-ft-) long *Kronosaurus* lived in the Early Cretaceous. It powered through the water after turtles and other plesiosaurs, snapping them up in its huge jaws.

Built for Speed

Pliosaurs had muscular bodies, short necks, and long heads. The short tail kept them streamlined and they swam by moving all four flippers at once. They were fast-moving and usually outswam prey. Once they had caught their victim, they shook it in their jaws and swallowed it whole.

Pliosaurs are named after the Late Jurassic marine reptile, *Pliosaurus*.

Kronosaurus's teeth were not very sharp, but they were good at gripping and crushing prey.

DID YOU KNOW? *Kronosaurus* was named after **Cronos,** the leader of the Titans in Greek mythology. Cronos's son, Zeus, became the king of the gods.

The pointed tail helped the body slip through the water without creating any drag.

History of Discovery

The first *Kronosaurus* fossils—teeth dug up in Australia in 1899—were not identified as *Kronosaurus* until the 1920s. For decades the pliosaur was known only in Australia. In 1994, paleontologists announced that a fossil had been found in Colombia, South America. *Kronosaurus* probably lived in shallow seas worldwide.

Pliosaurs "flew" through the water using their four wing-like flippers.

Kronosaurus's longest teeth were around 30 cm (11.8 in) long. Even the shortest were more than 7 cm (2.8 in).

PERIOD	TRIASSIC	JURASSIC	CRETACEOUS	AGE OF MAMMALS	
MILLIONS OF YEARS AGO	251	206	145	65	present

112

Name: *Kronosaurus* (KROH–nuh–SAWR–us)
Family: Pliosauridae
Length: 10 m (33 ft)
Weight: 8.2 tonnes (9 tons)

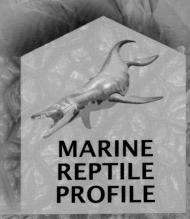

MARINE REPTILE PROFILE

Albertonectes

The elasmosaurs were plesiosaurs that had incredibly long necks. *Albertonectes* ("Alberta swimmer") had the longest neck of any elasmosaur, and the greatest overall body length of any plesiosaur.

Sneaky Skills

Albertonectes was not a fast swimmer, but it had a clever hunting technique. It approached shoals of fish from below, then let its head spring up on its long neck like a jack-in-the-box. This took the fish completely by surprise, so *Albertonectes* could gulp plenty down before they swam away.

Long-Necked Family

Elasmosaurs are named after the Late Cretaceous plesiosaur *Elasmosaurus*, but may have been around from the Late Triassic. Early elasmosaurs were just 3 m (9.8 ft) long. Elasmosaur means "thin-plated lizard" and refers to the thin plates in the reptiles' pelvic girdles.

Albertonectes' neck was about 7 m (23 ft) long—half of its total body length.

Elasmosaurus had stones called gastroliths (page 44) in its stomach to help it digest its food.

Albertonectes had a flat skull and long, pointed teeth.

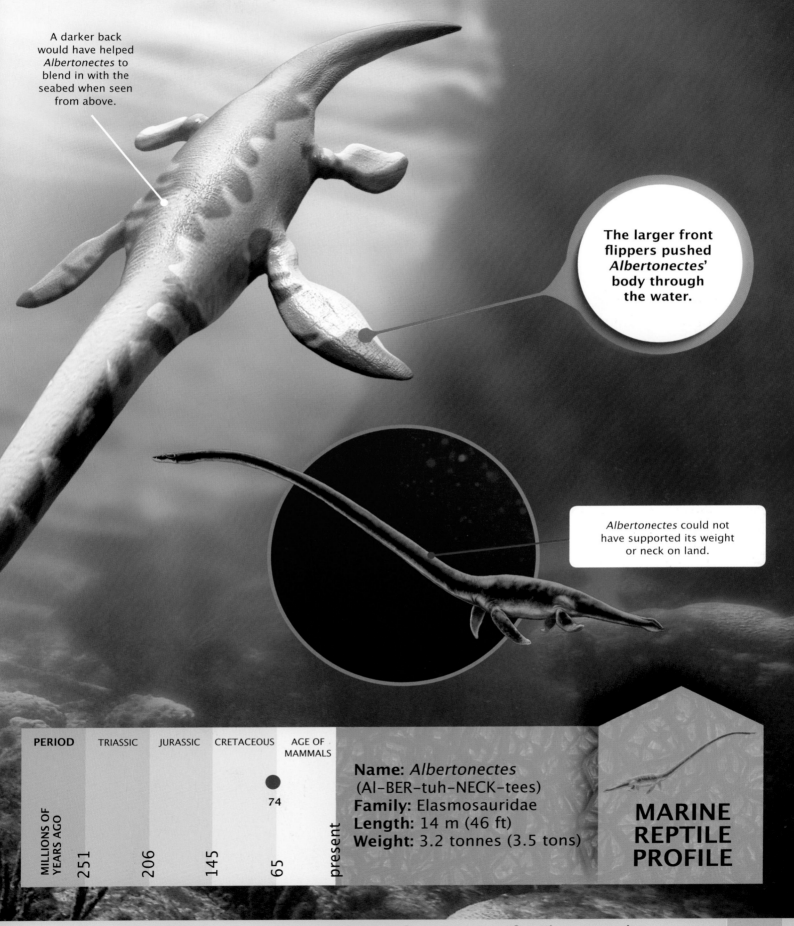

A darker back would have helped *Albertonectes* to blend in with the seabed when seen from above.

The larger front flippers pushed *Albertonectes'* body through the water.

Albertonectes could not have supported its weight or neck on land.

PERIOD	TRIASSIC	JURASSIC	CRETACEOUS	AGE OF MAMMALS	
MILLIONS OF YEARS AGO	251	206	145	65	present

74

Name: *Albertonectes*
(Al–BER–tuh–NECK–tees)
Family: Elasmosauridae
Length: 14 m (46 ft)
Weight: 3.2 tonnes (3.5 tons)

MARINE REPTILE PROFILE

DID YOU KNOW? *Albertonectes* is known from just one fossil—a complete skeleton that was found by **miners**. The discovery was announced in 2012.

Mosasaurus

The mosasaurs were the apex marine predators in the Late Cretaceous. They are named after *Mosasaurus*, an 18-m- (59-ft-) long hunter that went after fish, turtles, plesiosaurs, ichthyosaurs… and even smaller mosasaurs.

All in the Family

The smallest mosasaurs were less than 1 m (3.3 ft) long. Like *Mosasaurus*, they had lizard-shaped bodies and long, broad tails that helped to propel them through the water. Another family characteristic was giving birth to live young, rather than coming ashore to lay eggs.

The scales on the skin were tiny, making *Mosasaurus* smooth and streamlined.

Early Discoveries

The first known mosasaur remains were fragments of *Mosasaurus* skull found in the 1760s near Maastricht, in the Netherlands. It was mistaken for a toothed whale, and not identified as a reptile until 1799. The animal was finally named in 1822: *Mosasaurus* means "Mass River lizard," referring to the river that flows through the city of Maastricht.

The first *Mosasaurus* fossil was found in a chalk quarry.

PERIOD	TRIASSIC	JURASSIC	CRETACEOUS	AGE OF MAMMALS
MILLIONS OF YEARS AGO	251	206	145	65 · 68 · present

Name: *Mosasaurus* (MOH–suh–SAWR–us)
Family: Mosasauridae
Length: 18 m (59 ft)
Weight: 5 tonnes (5.5 tons)

MARINE REPTILE PROFILE

The skull was 1.7 m (5.6 ft) long—about the length of a family car.

Mosasaurus had a double-hinged jaw, like a snake's, that could open wide to swallow prey whole.

Five *Mosasaurus* species have been identified. This skull belongs to *Mosasaurus lemonnieri*, discovered in 1889.

Mosasaurus's paddle-like limbs each had five digits.

DID YOU KNOW? Paleontologists cannot agree if *Mosasaurus* was more closely related to snakes or to **monitor lizards**.

Dimorphodon

The pterosaurs, or "winged lizards," were flying reptiles that appeared in the Late Triassic, around 200 mya. *Dimorphodon* was an average-sized pterosaur that lived during the Early Jurassic. Its head looked like a puffin's.

Coastal Lifestyle

Dimorphodon could fly, but not for long distances. It probably lived along coasts, climbing cliffs or moving about on all fours. It caught its main food—insects—by snapping its jaws shut very fast. It also ate fish, small animals, and carrion.

This drawing of *Dimorphodon*'s skull appeared in Richard Owen's *A History of British Fossil Reptiles* (1849–84).

Wings and Flight

Pterosaurs were the first vertebrates (animals with backbones) that were capable of powered flight. Their wings, which were made of skin, muscle, and other tissues, stretched from their long fourth finger down to their ankles.

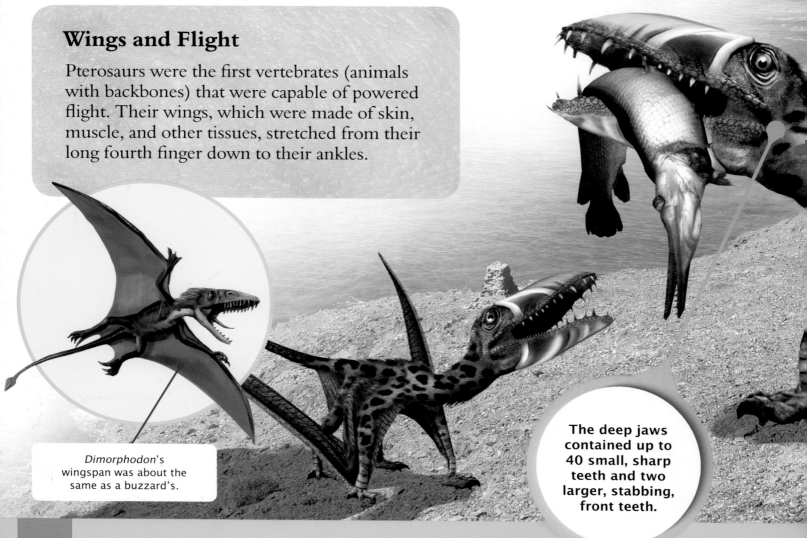

Dimorphodon's wingspan was about the same as a buzzard's.

The deep jaws contained up to 40 small, sharp teeth and two larger, stabbing, front teeth.

PERIOD	TRIASSIC	JURASSIC	CRETACEOUS	AGE OF MAMMALS	
MILLIONS OF YEARS AGO	251	206	145	65	present

193

Name: *Dimorphodon*
(Dye–MAW–fuh–don)
Family: Dimorphodontidae
Length: 1 m (3.3 ft)
Wingspan: 1.4 m (4.6 ft)
Weight: 2.3 kg (5 lb)

PTEROSAUR PROFILE

A diamond–shaped flap at the end of *Dimorphodon*'s tail helped it to steer when flying.

Dimorphodon may have cared for its young like this, or it may have left them to fend for themselves.

Dimorphodon had two types of teeth (its name means "two teeth shapes").

DID YOU KNOW? Fossil collector **Mary Anning** found the first *Dimorphodon* fossils in Dorset, southern England, in 1828.

Pterodactylus

Non-experts often use "pterodactyl" to mean any pterosaur, probably because *Pterodactylus* was the first-known pterosaur. It was discovered in Bavaria, Germany, in limestone formed in the Late Jurassic. More than 100 specimens have been found, many of them juveniles.

Breeding Season

Paleontologists have identified *Pterodactylus* that are one, two, and three years old. Their finds show that the reptile had a set breeding season, timed so eggs hatched when the conditions were best for raising young. *Pterodactylus* probably nested in colonies, like many seabirds today.

Pterodactylus was lightly built, with long wings. It would have been a powerful flier.

Pterodactylus had a crest of soft tissue on the top of its head for display. It kept growing throughout its life.

PERIOD	TRIASSIC	JURASSIC	CRETACEOUS	AGE OF MAMMALS
MILLIONS OF YEARS AGO	251	206 ● 150	145	65 present

Name: *Pterodactylus*
(Ter–oh–DAK–til–us)
Family: Pterodactylidae
Length: 80 cm (31.5 in)
Wingspan: 1 m (3.3 ft)
Weight: 4.6 kg (10 lb)

PTEROSAUR PROFILE

DID YOU KNOW? In the early 19th century, some people thought that *Pterodactylus* was a **marine amphibian**, and that its wings were really flippers.

Early Fossil Finds

Pterodactylus was discovered in 1784, but not recognized as a flying reptile until 1812. Its name means "winged finger." As in all pterosaurs, *Pterodactylus*'s wing was made up of stretched skin, attached to its extra-long fourth finger.

When *Pterodactylus* dived for fish, the hair-like pycnofibers around its neck stopped it getting cold and wet.

A young *Pterodactylus*, preserved in limestone.

The jaw contained up to 90 small, sharp teeth.

The wing was made up of skin and muscle.

Tropeognathus

With a wingspan as long as a school bus, *Tropeognathus* was one of the largest-known pterosaurs. It lived off the coast of what is now South America during the Early Cretaceous.

Spoon-Shaped Snout

Tropeognathus means "keel jaw." The name comes from the crests on the pterosaur's snout and lower jaw, which are shaped like keels (the steering fins on the bottom of a boat). The result is a curvy mouth that slides easily into the water to grab fish.

The rounded snout crests were probably used for display, to show off to possible mates or rivals.

The stretchy skin of the wing was supported by the pterosaur's long wrist bone and the long bones of the fourth finger.

PERIOD	TRIASSIC	JURASSIC	CRETACEOUS	AGE OF MAMMALS	present
MILLIONS OF YEARS AGO	251	206	145	65	

Name: *Tropeognathus*
(TRO–pe–oh–NA–thus)
Family: Pterodactylidae
Length: 6 m (20 ft)
Wingspan: 8.2 m (27 ft)
Weight: 13 kg (27 lb)

PTEROSAUR PROFILE

Shared Skies

Anhanguera was another large South American pterosaur, though not quite as giant as *Tropeognathus*. Its wingspan was about 4.5 m (15 ft). It lived a little later, about 96 mya, but had a similar lifestyle to *Tropeognathus*. It cruised close to shores, swooping down to snatch fish from the sea.

Anhanguera had crested snouts, too.

Tropeognathus had sharp, gappy teeth for spearing fish.

The snout was shaped like the keel of a boat.

DID YOU KNOW? *Tropeognathus* and *Anhanguera* were both **ornithocheirids**—pterosaurs with large wingspans that were specially adapted for flying out at sea.

Pteranodon

With its long, sharp beak and backward-pointing crest, the large pterosaur *Pteranodon* was the perfect shape for diving into the sea. It lived across what is now North America about 83 mya. It may also have lived in the area of Sweden, northern Europe.

Feeding Technique

Earlier pterosaurs such as *Pterodactylus* (pages 118–119) had teeth in their jaws, but *Pteranodon* had a toothless beak (its name means "wing without tooth"). A powerful flier, *Pteranodon* could have fed by diving headfirst into the water like a gannet, by dipping for food as it flew low over the sea, or by swimming and snatching fish near the surface.

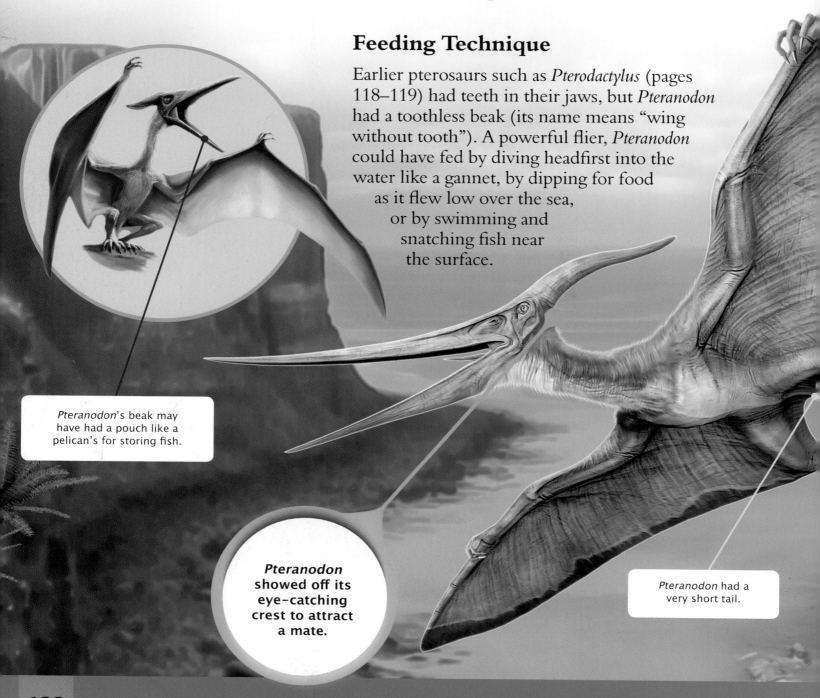

Pteranodon's beak may have had a pouch like a pelican's for storing fish.

Pteranodon showed off its eye-catching crest to attract a mate.

Pteranodon had a very short tail.

Unique Pterosaur

Pteranodon was the first pterosaur discovered outside Europe. Its wing bones were found in Kansas, U.S.A., in 1870. Over the years many different species were identified, but today most paleontologists agree that there was just one, *Pteranodon longiceps* (*longiceps* means "long-headed" and refers to the bony crest).

Pteranodon glided when it could, to save energy, but it also flapped its wings when it needed to put on a burst of speed.

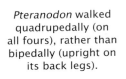

Pteranodon walked quadrupedally (on all fours), rather than bipedally (upright on its back legs).

PERIOD	TRIASSIC	JURASSIC	CRETACEOUS	AGE OF MAMMALS
MILLIONS OF YEARS AGO	251	206	145	65 · 83	present

Name: *Pteranodon* (Ter–AN–oh–don)
Family: Pteranodontidae
Length: 1.8 m (6 ft)
Wingspan: 6 m (20 ft)
Weight: 25 kg (55 lb)

PTEROSAUR PROFILE

DID YOU KNOW? More fossils have been found of *Pteranodon* than of any other pterosaur—at least **1,200** at the last count.

Quetzalcoatlus

Named after Quetzalcoatl, the feathered serpent god of Aztec mythology, *Quetzalcoatlus* lived at the end of the Cretaceous. Its wingspan was up to 11 m (36 ft), making it the largest of the 150 known species of pterosaur.

On the Lookout

Quetzalcoatlus had a long neck and good eyesight. On land it walked on all fours, looking for carrion or small animals to eat. Flight used a lot of energy. Wherever possible, *Quetzalcoatlus* glided rather than flapping its wings.

The wing membrane was thin but tough; it was just 23 cm (8 in) thick at the elbows.

Taking Off

Smaller pterosaurs could launch themselves into the air by running along on their back legs, like birds. Larger ones, such as *Quetzalcoatlus*, were too heavy for that and needed to start from a quadrupedal position. Their front legs were much stronger than their back ones, and could give enough of an upward thrust to make the animal airborne.

Pterosaurs did not have feathers. However some, perhaps including *Quetzalcoatlus*, had fuzzy filaments called pycnofibers covering their bodies.

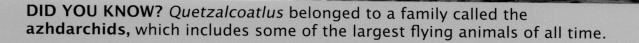

DID YOU KNOW? *Quetzalcoatlus* belonged to a family called the **azhdarchids,** which includes some of the largest flying animals of all time.

PERIOD	TRIASSIC	JURASSIC	CRETACEOUS	AGE OF MAMMALS	
MILLIONS OF YEARS AGO	251	206	145	65	present

67

Name: *Quetzalcoatlus*
(Kwet–zel–KWAT–al–us)
Family: Azhdarchidae
Height: 4.9 m (16 ft)
Wingspan: 11 m (36 ft)
Weight: 225 kg (496 lb)

PTEROSAUR PROFILE

Quetzalcoatlus flew inland, rather than over the sea, so it could glide on thermals (currents of warm air).

Quetzalcoatlus's narrow, toothless beak was at least 2.5 m (8 ft) long.

The back legs were probably the first to touch the ground when *Quetzalcoatlus* landed.

Glossary

ALLOSAUR
A large theropod with a long, narrow skull, usually with ornamental horns or crests.

AMMONITE
An extinct Mesozoic shellfish with a coiled shell.

ANKYLOSAUR
A thyreophoran with defensive osteoderms and, sometimes, a tail club.

ARCHOSAUR
An animal whose skull has one hole between the eye socket and nostril and another at the back of the lower jaw. Dinosaurs, pterosaurs, crocodiles, and birds are all archosaurs.

AZHDARCHID
A pterosaur with long legs, a long neck, and a huge wingspan.

BIOCHRON
A layer of rock named after the fossil animal or plant that most commonly occurs in it.

BIPEDAL
Walking upright on the back legs.

BROWSE
To feed on shoots, leaves, and other plant matter.

CARNIVORE
A meat-eater.

CARRION
Rotting flesh from a dead animal.

CERATOPSIAN
A marginocephalian with (usually) horns and frills. Early species were bipedal; later ones were large and quadrupedal.

CRETACEOUS PERIOD
The time from 145 to 65 mya, and the third of the periods that make up the Mesozoic era.

DIPLODOCID
A very long sauropod with relatively short legs.

DROMAEOSAUR
A small theropod with an outsize claw on each back foot.

EVOLUTION
The process by which one species changes into another over millions of years, by passing on particular characteristics from one generation to the next.

EXTINCT
Describes an animal or plant that has disappeared forever.

FLIPPER
A flat limb that has evolved to help an animal swim.

FOSSIL
The remains of an animal or plant that died long ago, preserved in rock.

FRILL
A bony area around a dinosaur's neck.

GASTROLITH
A stone in the stomach that helps digestion.

HADROSAUR
Also known as a duck-billed dinosaur, an ornithopod with an especially beak-like mouth.

HERBIVORE
A plant-eater.

ICHTHYOSAUR
A dolphin-like, predatory marine reptile of the Mesozoic.

IGUANODONTID
A large, plant-eating ornithopod.

JURASSIC PERIOD
The time from 206 to 145 mya, and the second of the periods that make up the Mesozoic era.

MARGINOCEPHALIAN
An ornithischian dinosaur with thicker bone at the back of the skull.

MESOZOIC ERA
The period of geological time from 251 to 65 million years ago.

MOSASAUR
A large, predatory marine reptile of the Cretaceous, which had four paddle-like limbs.

MYA
Short for "millions of years ago."

NODOSAUR
An ankylosaur with bumps and spikes on its skull, but no tail club.

NOTHOSAUR
A marine reptile of the Triassic, with webbed, paddle-like feet.

OMNIVORE
An animal that eats plants and meat.

ORNITHISCHIAN
Describes dinosaurs with hip bones arranged like a bird's. All plant-eaters, they include ornithopods, marginocephalians, and thyreophorans.

ORNITHOCHEIRID
A pterosaur with a huge wingspan and keel-shaped snout.

ORNITHOPOD
An ornithischian dinosaur with a bony, beak-like mouth.

OSTEODERM
A lumpy scale on a reptile's skin.

PACHYCEPHALOSAUR
A bipedal marginocephalian with a thick skull.

PALEONTOLOGIST
A scientist who studies fossils.

PLATE
A protective, bony section on a reptile's skin.

PLESIOSAUR
A long-necked, predatory marine reptile that lived in the Jurassic and Cretaceous.

PLIOSAUR
A kind of plesiosaur with a short neck and big head.

PREDATOR
An animal that hunts and eats other animals for food.

PREY
An animal that is hunted and eaten by other animals for food.

PROSAUROPOD
A primitive sauropod.

PTEROSAUR
A flying reptile with wings made from skin stretched over a long fourth finger.

PYCNOFIBER
A hair-like body covering found on a pterosaur's body.

QUADRUPEDAL
Walking on all four legs.

RHYNCHOSAUR
A small, primitive reptile.

SAURISCHIAN
Describes dinosaurs with hip bones arranged like a lizard's. They include the meat-eating theropods and plant-eating sauropods.

SAUROPOD
An enormous, long-necked, plant-eating saurischian dinosaur that walked on all fours.

SCAVENGE
To eat carrion or leftover kills from other hunters.

SERRATED
Having a notched, knife-like edge.

SPECIES
One particular type of living thing. Members of the same species look similar and can produce offspring together.

SPINOSAUR
A specialist theropod with a long, narrow snout for eating fish.

STEGOSAUR
A thyreophoran with defensive bony plates on its back.

SYNAPSID
A primitive mammal.

THAGOMIZER
The group of defensive spikes on a stegosaur's tail.

THERIZINOSAUR
A large (probably plant-eating) theropod with huge hand claws.

THEROPOD
A bipedal saurischian dinosaur with sharp teeth and claws.

THYREOPHORAN
An ornithischian dinosaur with defensive osteoderms or plates.

TITANOSAUR
A huge sauropod with a relatively small head.

TRIASSIC PERIOD
The time from 251 to 206 mya, and the first of the periods that make up the Mesozoic era.

TROODONTID
A birdlike theropod with long legs and good senses.

TYRANNOSAUR
A large theropod with a huge head and relatively small arms.

WINGSPAN
The width of a flying animal's outstretched wings, from wing tip to wing tip.

Index